Rooted Together

A Mother -&- Daughter Rite of Passage

By
Jolene Witt

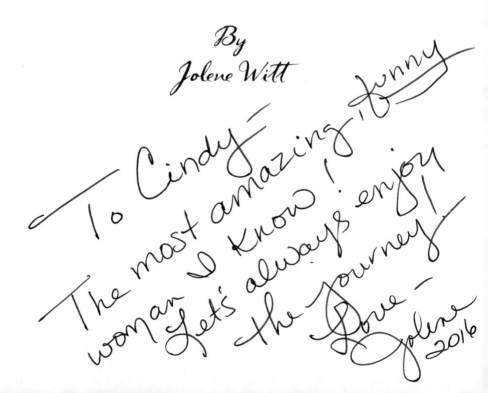

To Cindy —
The most amazing, funny
woman I know! .
Let's always enjoy
the journey!
Love —
Jolene
2016

For information, visit Moore Publishing at

www.MoorePublishingBooks.com

ISBN:# 978-0-9898764-0-7

I dedicate this book to all
those special women who have gone before us.
Those who have lived and told their stories,
and have given us the courage to live and tell our own.

Contents

Who are we?

My husband Dan and I have been blessed with three children, all girls. From the moment they were born, each has been spirited and fun, in their own unique and individual ways. That's not to say, that as parents, we haven't had our trying times too, hours and days when our patience ran thin and our tempers grew thick. Over the past twenty-three years, we've lived and learned much as a family. Through it all, I can honestly say, the five of us have enjoyed one wild and wonderful ride.

With the birth of each daughter, my husband often found himself on the receiving end of some light-hearted teasing. He was often jabbed in the ribs by one of his guy friends asking, "So, you're gonna go back and try for that boy, right?"

Dan always took the joking in stride, but would also answer, "Nah, I'm just happy this one's here and healthy."

In the dark of night, when he and I would lie in our bed, listening to our daughter's soft and rhythmic breathing through the baby monitor pointed towards our attentive ears, he'd hold my hand and tell me how happy he was—and how thankful he felt for our newest little girl sleeping just across the hall. Then he would begin to describe for me his plans of teaching her how to hunt and how to bait a hook, to mow the lawn and to drive a boat. Over the years, he did all these things, and so much more.

We had the luxury of raising our girls on the family farm, in a time before cell phones became the fourth commonly used utensil at dinner tables and Facebook friends replaced the ones living down the road. As our girls grew, they played outside—barefoot in the summer and bundled up in the winter. During the spring rains, they spent hours stomping in mud puddles, and when those dried up, they scrambled to their secret hideout: the ditch bank under the bridge at the edge of our property. If the summer sun grew too intense, they stretched out beneath the shade trees in our backyard. And when Mother Michigan decided to dump her winter coat, they played King of the Hill high on top of our ever-growing snow piles.

Every summer we took a simple, one-week vacation, to the northern part of our state, once the fields had been planted and we were waiting for the sprouts to appear. In the fall, Dan and I walked our girls through the woodlot down the road, and marveled as the trees magically turned from green to crimson red, buttery yellow and burnt orange. We went sledding in the winter, and canoeing in the spring. And while all these seasons passed, gently and without much notice, our girls grew.

When their school days arrived and one-by-one they began boarding the big yellow bus, I was lucky enough to land a job in our local school system, working mostly part-time and enjoying the same holidays and summer breaks they did. Dan and I relished their endearing elementary years and we survived the bumpy, jagged middle school ones. By high school, each of our girls had acquired a strong sense of who she was, and a small handful of really good friends.

Our daughters all played sports, but mostly for fun; they knew they'd never be the star-athlete, and they were content inside that truth. They worked hard for their grades and along the way, they discovered their own hidden talents and personal passions. Cote, the oldest, uncovered a deep love for creating art. Hannah, our middle child, found expression through the written word, and Josie, the youngest, realized she had a voice that could sing her heart out. They were never the most popular, nor were they ever placed on that unrealistic and shaky pedestal of high school super-stardom—and for that, Dan and I sighed in relief. We witnessed enough topples and tip-overs to know this wasn't a safe and sensible place for them to be.

Our girls grew up adored by their grandparents, though they lost both grandmothers at too-early an age. They were surrounded by numerous and clamorous aunts and uncles, and when the families all came together, our girls played and kept up with all their boy cousins, no matter the game or sport of choice.

I guess you could say our daughters had an old-fashioned kind of upbringing. While we never consciously talked about it, it was the kind of childhood my husband and I always hoped to give them. It wasn't easy to do, though. There were times we were tempted to give them too much too early, to hand over the keys to adulthood too soon. We made sure we said yes when they asked if they had to wear hand-me-downs, and no when they begged for a cell phone before the age of eighteen.

Being a parent is a tough job, and Dan and I are, by far, no experts in the field. All we know is that we did the best we could. We loved our girls and guided them through the early years, so they could be faithful and fruitful in the later ones. We also know we're not done yet. So, we press on, with one lifelong, and optimistic hope: that our three daughters—Cote, Hannah, and Josie—never forget where they came from, and always, always remember we're right behind them, wherever they may go.

The Journey Begins

What you are about to read is the story of a mother and her eighteen-year-old daughter who travel over five thousand miles to climb a tree on the Oregon Coast. Throughout their two-week, cross-country adventure, they will learn more about themselves and each other than they ever dreamed possible. However, this story needs to start at the beginning, and to do that we must go back almost two years before Cote and I ever buckled our seat belts. That's when this all started—when our mother-daughter rite of passage truly began.

It was a wintry day in January 2008, and I had stumbled upon an article in my latest issue of *Women's Health* magazine. It was a "You Can Do This" piece, from the monthly column designed to challenge the reader to push herself, both physically and mentally, to new heights and past self-imposed limits. January's challenge happened to describe climbing out on the limb of a 250-foot Douglas fir. The glossy, full-color picture gracing the page in front of me stopped my fingers from flipping any farther through the magazine that day. I couldn't believe my eyes. Never before had I seen such a beautiful tree, and not even in my wildest dreams had I ever considered climbing one.

I devoured the article, word-for-word. When I finished, I looked over at my oldest daughter, the one who had loved to climb trees since she'd been tall enough to grasp the bottom branches by tiptoeing on wobbly step stools, and said these words now famous in our family, "Someday you and I are going to climb real trees." I held up the article, with great pride and boldness, so she could see how serious I was.

Like any normal, enthusiastic, open-minded sixteen-year-old, she looked at me and said, "Yeah, right Mom."

Despite her skepticism, something happened that day. The seed of an idea was planted, and in the days that followed it took root and began to grow. I tore the article out of the magazine and placed it in its own special folder. Every so often I referred back to the author's incredible account of what it was like to climb these massive beauties. I didn't know when or how, but I knew someday Cote and I would have our own tree-climbing story to tell. It would be a version lived and breathed and retold by us, to those willing to listen.

The day I tucked the article away, I tucked a few dollars into a plain white envelope as well. I did this almost without thinking, and then started adding to it whenever I could. A ten-dollar bill leftover at the end of the month, or a twenty I could pretend I never had, was slipped inside the pouch. On the outside of the envelope, I wrote these words by John Muir: *In every walk with nature one receives far more than he seeks.* I knew someday Cote and I would walk into a forest glade far from home, and find answers to questions we didn't even know we were asking. The roads taking us there would be filled with adventure and riddled with unknowns. Yet, deep in my heart, I knew the journey could prove vital to our mother-daughter relationship. We stood to uncover truths about ourselves, about each other, and about what our future might hold in-store.

So, what happened next?

Well, to be honest, not much. For the next eighteen months, the hustle and bustle of everyday life offered little time for us to speak of climbing trees. It was only on rare occasions that we threw comments over our shoulders as we passed each other in the hall, reminding one another "someday" still loomed somewhere out on the horizon. There was no time to do much else, for there was too much other stuff to do. Cote was knee-deep in her senior year of high school, and I was in deep trying to keep up. Each day was a mini-milestone that needed to be savored, despite its bittersweet taste. There was the last snap of her senior pictures and her final night of float building. I cheered as Cote bumped, set, and spiked her last volleyball, and murmured a silent prayer as she took her final shot from the free-throw line. My breath caught in my throat as she came down the stairs dressed for her senior prom, and tears pooled in the corners of my eyes when she walked up the aisle in her cap and gown.

With each passing day, I felt the childlike grasp Cote once kept tight on my hand beginning to loosen. She was unlacing her fingers from mine, slowly and surely, indicating change was in the air. It fell upon us softly that year, along with the autumn leaves, the winter snow, and the springtime showers. And then one day it hit me—soon our lives would be changing forever. Cote was to leave for college the following fall, and who we were, who we had always been, would fade like our evening shadows into the night.

That's when the ticking of an invisible clock started pounding in my ear. The countdown was well underway, and I needed to race and catch up. Before long, Cote would be decorating a tiny, dorm-size home and exploring a massive, campus-size backyard. She would be out in the world, standing on her own, and making choices without the benefit of her mother's endless supply of advice. Was she ready for all this? Was I?

Suddenly tree-climbing became urgent. Imperative. Critical. It was no longer just about climbing 250 feet up into the air. It was about a mother and daughter taking a journey that would weave them together in a way that could withstand the test of time. This rite of passage would allow us the opportunity to open our eyes, our hearts, and our voices to what needed to be seen, what needed to be felt, and what desperately needed to be said. To do this, we needed time uninterrupted, free from all distractions, in order to talk about life, love, relationships, and believing in one's dreams. Cote and I needed time to explore who we really were and who we were going to become. More than anything, we needed time.

So, our tree-climbing conversations turned serious. We quickly narrowed down the "when"—August 2009, four weeks before Cote left for college. The "how" on the other hand, proved a bit more challenging. I had always assumed we would fly to the West Coast. It would make our trip shorter, easier, and much more manageable. It wasn't until a lazy Sunday afternoon in March 2009, that I discovered my daughter had a totally different mode of transportation in mind. She wanted to drive.

"DRIVE??!! Drive to Oregon? Cote, do you realize what you're saying? It would take us twelve to fourteen days round-trip to do something like that! Think about it…fourteen days…in a car… alone…with just your mother!"

Her answer surprised me, then reminded me of what life is truly all about.

"Mom, it's not about just showing up and climbing a tree for me. It's about seeing everything along the way. It's about the whole journey, what it takes to get there. I want to see it all. I don't want to miss a thing."

I sat there stunned by her cool composure and solid response. Her eyes held such passion and hope and determination. She believed we could really do this, and I knew part of the reason why. For years, I had been encouraging all three of our daughters to "fully participate in life every day." In fact, I threw this phrase at them every chance that came along, hoping it would stick. Now my eldest daughter was sitting here, telling me she was ready to do just that. How could I be the one to tell her no, that it wasn't possible?

So, with our "how" finally decided upon, Cote and I picked the date of our departure—Sunday, August 2nd, at one o'clock in the afternoon. After studying the calendar, we realized this would give us two full weeks before life required us to be back home. Other than picking the date, no other formal planning went into our trip. That part was intentional. Cote's journey needed to match her spirited and wander-loving ways as much as possible. No schedule was committed on paper; no "must-do" ever penned in ink. We had wiggle room inside this adventure for wrong-turns and unexpected detours, which I knew would happen but also trusted would lead us right to where we were supposed to be. We circled our destination in red—Eugene, Oregon. Anything before or beyond that was a blank book. It was up to us to pen and paint its pearly white pages, to tell our own story. I knew there would be triumph and discovery, as well as challenges and disappointment. With my daughter at my side, I couldn't wait to experience them all.

This is the story of our journey, of Cote's rite of passage. It's time for us to buckle up and head our car west. I'm glad you're here, going along with us—and more than anything, I hope you enjoy the ride.

Author's Note: This trip did not materialize independently of conversations with Dan. In fact, many discussions took place between us prior to Cote and me driving cross-country. Although I left this part out, please know that these were important background conversations that held much merit and weight. Suffice it to say, I had his blessing before we left. I respected his concerns and heeded his advice. He, in turn, understood my reasons and fully supported every precious mother-daughter mile.

Day 1: Deerfield, Michigan to Davenport, Iowa, 412 miles

Let your heart be your map.
~ Hannah Witt, August, 2009

Cote and I pulled out of our driveway just after one o'clock in the afternoon, with the bright rays of sunshine pouring through our freshly washed windshield. We had spent the morning as a family, attending church and preparing for our departure. It seemed we had become a couple of "bag ladies," as the car was packed with duffle bags, book bags, and sleeping bags. We also tossed in two journals, a handful of pens, a fold-out map of the United States, a cooler of food, a camera, and an enthusiastic sense of adventure.

Despite the supplies packed into our backseat, the trip had yet to feel real. Cote and I were undeniably excited, but we had to admit that at first it felt as if we were only on our way to Toledo for a typical day of shopping. Not until we hit the turnpike and pointed our car west, did reality begin to set in. I quickly plucked our toll ticket from the mouth of the big metal box and then pressed the foot pedal to pick up speed. As I did, our bodies seemed to sigh in unison and slide more comfortably down into the cushions of our seats. It was hard to believe, but we were really, truly, on our way.

Light-hearted attitudes and easy-flowing conversations kept us company for a while, but before long, the miles and minutes began to stretch and pass by us in silence. We crossed the border into Indiana, then into Illinois, when somewhere along this stretch of highway, I had a mini-moment of panic. *What if the entire trip is like this? Long periods of time passing with nothing but silence and changing landscapes taking place around us and between us?*

As quickly as that fear grabbed me, I knew I had to let it go. I cracked open the window of my mind and let the eastbound breeze take it back to wherever it came from.

I knew Cote and myself far better than to waste another minute fearing something so benign. We had twelve long days ahead of us, with nothing but open roads and wide-open spaces. There was no need to whip out every question and conversation tucked inside the suitcases of our minds. Rushing into these things, would have felt forced and unnatural. We now had the time we needed and plenty of it. I sensed Cote and I were both using these first few hours to relax and breathe. We were emptying ourselves of all the distracting details we were leaving behind in order to absorb the magnitude of what was about to take place. Wiping the slate clean, we were readying ourselves for the lessons that would begin to arrive with tomorrow's sunrise.

Since we had topped off our gas tank in Toledo, our gauge didn't read *50 miles until empty* until we reached the sprawling cornfields of Princeton, Illinois. I was actually surprised when the warning light flickered on. Until now, I hadn't thought about being the only acting parent on this 5,000-mile adventure. Without my husband occupying the seat beside me, the full weight of all car care and maintenance rested solely upon my shoulders. Realizing this and our situation, while seeing nothing but fields of green spread out in front of us, I petitioned Cote to pray for a quick-appearing gas station. Then I made a mental note to check the gauge more regularly. Fortunately, a filling station was waiting for us just minutes down the road.

Despite our easy-going first day of driving, seven hours didn't pass without one major mother-daughter discussion. The topic? *The Do's and Don'ts of Texting, 101.*

Cote and I stumbled into this conversation quite by accident, stemming from the simple fact that she had the latest and greatest in cell phone technology, and I didn't. Her phone could easily supply five full bars of reception from any location and hold a charge that would last for days. Mine, on the other hand, could be plugged in for eighteen hours straight and only allow me one five-minute phone call before dying again. Cote's phone could take messages, pictures, and accurately calculate a fifteen percent tip on any food bill. Mine only told me that I missed a call—not even from whom. Hers, of course, could send and receive text messages, while my phone had nothing more than a number pad with a screen big enough to show me the ten digits I was dialing.

It was during this cell phone comparison that our conversation turned to the etiquette of texting in today's high-tech society. Cote and I shared our personal opinions on what seemed right, what felt wrong, what we thought was acceptable, and what we believed crossed the line of rudeness when using this modern form of communication. The generation gap between us widened as I expressed my long list of texting negatives and Cote countered with her own extensive column of positives. In the end, she conceded that in the company of certain people (mainly her mother), it was rude to text or check for a text. In return, I agreed that texting was a viable form of communicating with friends both far and near. I even went so far as to acknowledge that her generation would surely be expected to use this method of technology both skillfully and efficiently in the business world of tomorrow.

About the time we crossed the Mississippi River, our cell

phone and texting code-of- etiquette conversation took a deeper turn. I asked Cote to stop and think about the message she might inadvertently send if she texted while in the presence of someone else. I wasn't referring to the message she was typing with her thumbs and sending with the click of a keypad. Instead, I was asking her to think about the message she would be sending nonverbally to the person who was standing before her.

"If you stop the flow of face-to-face friendship, in order to 'talk' to the invisible face at the other end of your tiny keyboard, then what are you really saying, Cote?" Not really expecting a response, I answered my own question. "You're telling the person you're with, 'You're not enough for me. I'm going to put some of my time and attention over here.' What's more, you are placing yourself in two locations at once—something that not too long ago used to be impossible to do, and for a good reason. If you divide yourself between two places, you can't really be fully present in the magical moment of either. You'll end up with a chunk of time that has been sliced and diced and split apart. And in the end, all you'll have to show for your dual communicating is a handful of text messages that could have waited and an opportunity lost forever to be one-on-one with the person you're with."

Cote stomached my well-intended soapbox speech with a respect rarely found in the youth of today. She listened without interruption and even showed signs of great thought and contemplation after my closing argument. I decided not to push my luck, so I turned my attention back to the open road, letting my final statement rest in the space between us. We drove as far as Davenport, Iowa, before we pulled over for the night at an American Inn motel. As we walked inside our room, Cote handed me two letters from loved ones back home, letters she had kept secret from me in her backpack.

"Sure. You get two letters, and I don't get anything. How do you like that?"

I turned my head away and smiled, for I had fourteen secret letters of my own, written by fourteen incredible and important women in Cote's life back home. Months ago, I asked them to write some words of inspiration, some life advice, to share with Cote while on her rite of passage. They didn't let me down. I had their letters safely squirreled away inside my backpack, waiting to be handed out one-by-one over the next twelve days.

I decided to leave Cote empty-handed a little longer, while I read and savored my own unexpected words of encouragement. I waited until after she had taken her shower and finished her last bite of Chinese take-out. I kept the letters hidden as she posted our location on Facebook and sent goodnight text messages to her girlfriends back home. Then, just before she turned out the light on this first day of her rite of passage, I tossed a sealed envelope upon her bed. Cote let out a whoop of delight, grabbed the precious gift, and hugged it to her chest. Her fingers eagerly tore open the seal and retrieved the note hand-written by her Aunt Cathy. The room grew silent as Cote fell under the spell of reading from this ancient form of communication. A smile spread slowly across her face, and as it did, I couldn't help but smile too.

Day 2: Davenport, Iowa to Sydney, Nebraska, 692 miles

Make it through Nebraska by the end of the day,
if you can.
~ Josh Seidell, August 3, 2009, 10:42 a.m.

Cote and I did our best to follow Josh's advice, but when all was said and done, we fell short by one hundred miles. We left Davenport, Iowa, at 8:30 in the morning, with fresh ice in our cooler and a hot cup of McDonald's coffee in my hand. Despite our staunch intentions to avoid any particular must-do on this rite of passage, we did have one unexpected opportunity arise that was just too good to pass up on.

A few days earlier, my sister and nephew had left Yellowstone National Park to begin their own cross-country trek. They were heading east towards home. Josh had spent his summer working at a hotel inside this vast outdoor nature reserve, and Debbie had gone to fetch him, now that the job was over. My nephew had spent the previous sixty days hiking and exploring a place Cote and I hoped to visit on our own return trip home. We were sure he would have some incredible stories to share. Now, through a few well-timed phone calls, we determined that our paths would cross today somewhere along Interstate-80.

Our overlapping point turned out to be Iowa City at ten o'clock in the morning. A McDonald's was just off the exit, so we pulled into the parking lot for an hour of coffee and conversation inside the restaurant.

The four of us found it strange to meet up in a place so random, so far from home. Aunt Deb and Josh asked about our adventure, our plans, and climbing trees. We asked them about Yellowstone and what we should see if we only had two hours to spend inside the park on our way back home. Josh's advice was pointed and priceless, "If you only have two hours in Yellowstone, here's what you do: drive inside the park and find a huge boulder. Stop the car, walk over to that boulder and sit down on it. Then put your head in your hands and start crying, because you only have two hours to spend in Yellowstone."

I had no doubt his words were wise and true, but since Cote and I had made a pact early on that our journey steer clear of any set schedule, we accepted Josh's advice and then let it go. We knew we couldn't worry about how much time we'd have in places we hadn't even visited yet. Nor could we allow our minds to pitch so far forward in some feeble attempt to mold and shape the outcome of this rite of passage. Our goal was to simply live the moment at hand—the one we had been given right now. In many ways, I believed this was a good recipe to follow, no matter what date happened to be on the calendar.

After we said our goodbyes, Cote and I jumped back onto I-80 West, where cornfields and cattle dotted our landscape for the next nine hours. The tranquil scenery led to a peaceful car ride, and once again, we drifted in and out of contented silence. Cote snapped pictures, left and right, mostly of nothing much at all. She seemed determined to digitally mark the minutes, to faithfully record the road. Around two o'clock in the afternoon, she took over the driving, owning the next one hundred miles of Nebraska, while I angled my seat back and closed my weary eyes.

Two hours later, the town of Kearny came into view. We both perked up as the city offered us something to look at besides green fields and blue sky. We decided to take the exit, grab a snack at Taco Bell, and hunt down the Museum of Nebraskan Art. The billboard had caught Cote's eye a mile or two back, and while it sounded as exciting to me as another cornfield, for her it held both intrigue and mystery. She insisted we pull over to investigate.

We drove into Kearny thinking there would be more signs to point our way to the museum, but one never appeared. In fact, all the way down Main Street there was no indication that the establishment even existed. We knew we could pull over to ask, but instead we decided to simply take our chances and ramble aimlessly through town to see if we could find it. Before long, Cote and I forgot all about the museum. It was the odd storefronts and peculiar business signs that distracted us and had us laughing like a couple of junior high schoolgirls. One storefront caught both Cote's fancy and funny bone: a huge white chicken perched above a neon sign advertising donuts. The oddity of the combination had my daughter doubled over in laughter, while hanging on to the dashboard, so as not to bump her head.

After about fifteen minutes and a very valiant attempt, we finally abandoned the hunt for the elusive museum and headed back to the interstate. When Cote and I entered the highway, I pushed the pedal a little harder, until we were going eighty miles per hour on I-80. Wide-open, flat green landscapes returned to greet us. However, now they were speckled with enormously large and slow-twirling windmills, the size of which I had never seen before.

They stood as giant aliens, row after row, glaring white against the endless soft fields of green. I watched their methodical movements, arms circling wide, making every effort to harness a power unseen in order to create a power within. Thoughts of my own spiritual journey surfaced in my mind, as the metaphor standing bold before me took hold. I, too, rely daily on a Power unseen to refuel my body and soul. This idea brought a quiet comfort, a sense of peace, and traveled with me for the next twenty-some miles.

Around Chappelle, Nebraska, Cote and I hit a late-in-the-day dust storm, which quickly turned into an early evening thunder and lightning show. It started with a few innocent tumbleweeds bouncing across the highway in front of us, entertaining enough at first to distract us from the darkening skies overhead and the rising winds. Soon, however, rain began pelting our car, blowing sideways across our windshield. We were shocked to see a storm so intense closing in on us. It came from every direction, leaving no way for us to outrun it. The heavy black clouds swiftly erased every last inch of clear blue Nebraskan sky we had grown accustomed to, and then we found ourselves immersed in a torrential downpour.

Still we pushed on, trying our best to reach and cross the western border of this expansive state before the day came to an end. Cote and I finally gave up, though, and handed Nebraska the victory when we pulled over in the town of Sydney. We were tired and spent. Going another mile was out of the question. The next town that appeared on our trusty fold-out map looked to be well over thirty miles on the other side of the Wyoming border, so Sydney looked like a heavenly oasis after our long day across the massive corn-fed desert. We found a simple motel, grabbed a fresh change of clothes and our backpacks, and then walked stiff-legged toward our room. Hot showers and take-out pizza were all we could think about.

Once we were clean and fed, Cote spent the last two hours of the evening on Facebook while I scribbled notes about our day in my journal. Around 11:00 p.m., she closed her laptop, so I set down my pen, thinking we were calling it a night. That was not to be the case. Instead of turning out the light, Cote turned and launched a topic at me that sent my head spinning. I had no idea the strong, spirited, and healthy esteemed young woman sitting before me, was being plagued by such a nasty, nagging question—a question that was chipping away at the pieces of her very soul.

"Why is it that some people seem to like me, and others do not? And why...why...can't I just say, 'Like me or don't. It's up to you and I don't care?'"

I knew instantly the shell of our rite of passage had officially been broken open. The easy-breezy weather that had blown us this far on our journey had been replaced by storm clouds of self-doubt and self-worth—storms that once again I didn't see coming.

I sat there for a moment, stunned at the glimpse Cote was giving me of her fragile, interior eighteen-year-old soul. The mother in me instinctively wanted to fight to protect her, so I had to bite my tongue against the age-old parental response, "How could anyone not like you?"

Instead, I took a deep breath and forced myself to remember who was sitting in front of me, opening her heart and trusting me with her fears. Cote was no longer a five-year-old little girl, having a spat with her best friend. She was a young woman trying to determine the steps she needed to take in order to define who she was in her own eyes, and who in turn, she stood to become in the eyes of others. I could not coo and coddle her. My daughter was searching for something more, and I felt honored to be the person she trusted enough to help her find the answers.

Cote's question was legitimate, and one I had asked myself many times before. In fact, I believe it's a question we all ask ourselves at some point in life. The answer isn't easy though, and it won't be the same for every person who asks. Tonight, however, it was my daughter doing the asking. So, I took another deep breath, put aside what hour it was, and offered Cote the space to open up further.

We talked well into the night as she described how certain people made her feel. I shared some personal experiences of my own. We finally concluded that when people seem to have a problem liking you, it isn't so much about *you* as it is about *them*. They are often the ones carrying around the heavy baggage that bogs them down and blocks their heart. Cote and I talked about finding the strength to stand in the truth of who we really are, in the midst of wherever we may be in life, and with whomever may be at our side.

Sleep eventually snuck up on us, quiet and thief-like. By the time our eyes closed and Cote and I drifted off to dream, our minds had found some rest. More importantly, our bond as mother and daughter had tightened. The well of trust and understanding between us had been dug deeper, filling my heart as I gave myself over to sleep.

Day 3: Sydney, Nebraska to Steamboat Springs, Colorado, 323 miles

This is a view to which nothing needs to be added...This scenery satisfies my soul.
~ Isabella Bird, 1879, A Lady's Life in the Rocky Mountains

Isabella Bird was right. The Rockies lacked absolutely nothing back in 1879, and I can confidently say they continue to lack for nothing today. As Cote and I explored these majestic mountains, my soul was more than satisfied!

This was my daughter's maiden voyage through the grandest of snow-capped peaks, and my second. My parents brought me here when I was young girl of twelve, some thirty-odd years ago. I remember being enchanted by the sheer size of these mountains as they towered over me. Today, not only did their size captivate me, but their indescribable beauty stunned me as well.

However, before I go on any further about the Rockies, I must first back up and write about how our morning unfolded.

Cote and I started the day by checking out the town of Sydney, Nebraska. Despite my desire to hit the highway and head for the hills, Cote insisted we first check out the Cabela's store located just down the road from our motel. She wanted to see how this original outdoor giant compared to its newer version, which had recently been constructed in Dundee, Michigan, a few short miles from our home back in Deerfield.

As we pulled into the parking lot, Cote was giddy and excited. With a single step inside the famous outdoor retailer, however, her enthusiasm quickly faded and all but disappeared. The place lacked both the size and swagger of its sibling store back home. There was no massive mountain teeming with taxidermy, no bubbling brook trickling with trout. There were only a few racks of clothes, some odd and ends in outdoor gear, and a couple of second-rate stuffed animals. Nevertheless, Cote set off to explore the store. She quickly rounded the racks, snapped a few silly shots, and even took a moment to ham it up with a freak-of-nature mannequin she found lounging in a floor model hammock.

By 9:30 a.m., we were back on the highway, driving towards Cheyenne. According to our map, we had a decent stretch of both time and miles before we reached the foothills of the Rockies, so I decided to unpack a couple of the questions I had brought along with me on this trip.

The topic concerned the fifteen-month relationship Cote had recently ended with her high school boyfriend. The breakup wasn't easy, but Cote knew it was necessary. The fit hadn't been right for a long time; the differences between them were obvious and difficult to deny. Finally, two weeks prior to pushing off on her rite of passage, Cote found the courage to break things off for good.

I knew my daughter was ready to move on, both mentally and emotionally, and she knew I completely supported her decision to end the relationship. What I didn't want, however, was for her to miss any life lesson that might be lingering in the wake of this split. I knew that in her rush to put her past behind her, Cote might end up dismissing the entire relationship without a second thought. Or even worse, she might come to think of the past fifteen months as a huge "waste of time." I didn't want either to happen.

I knew from my years of experience, every relationship, no matter how long it lasts, has the potential to bring something out, stir something up, or add something to your life. It may be a quick jolt of laughter or a long-term commitment. A relationship may alter your outlook on life, or create a new perspective within yourself. It could change the compass settings of where you're headed, or brush the fog from your view, unveiling a path that is surprisingly clearer than ever before. This long-term high school romance surely planted seeds of growth and maturity inside Cote. I didn't want the spouts to become raked over and buried under any adolescent mud and muck.

So, after carefully composing the questions inside my head, I turned to her and asked, "Cote, knowing what you know now, what will you look for in your next relationship? What are some of the qualities you liked about this guy? What are some that were missing for you?"

To my surprise, a floodgate of conversation opened up between us. Cote began by turning over some of the dirt of her own self-truths, cultivating the soil of her past year. She rooted around and found a few stray weeds, which together we identified and pulled from the ground of her soul. We talked about the good, the bad, the challenges, and the triumphs. We touched upon what she had learned, what she had liked, what she would repeat, and what she would leave behind.

As our heart-to-heart grew deeper, the mountains in the distance grew closer. Before we knew it, we had turned south on Highway 25 at Cheyenne and crossed over the Colorado border. We were headed for Trail Ridge Road, one of the most scenic routes through the Rocky Mountain National Forest.

It was just outside of Estes Park, an entranceway into the mountain range, that memories from my childhood came crashing through the attic doors of my mind. They hit me so hard, I actually had to pull over to the side of the road and stop the car.

The pictures were vivid and full of detail. It felt like I was sifting through a box of snapshots from a vacation taken so very long ago. The mountains looming before me sparked such long-lost memories that I had a sudden urge to call my dad back home. Sitting in front of the *Welcome to Estes Park* road sign, I dialed his number. After three short rings, my father's voice came on the line. I immediately said, "Dad, guess where I am."

To this day, I don't know how he did it, but he guessed exactly right. "You're just about ready to drive into the Rockies."

With overflowing enthusiasm, I confirmed his answer. Then, my dad immediately began painting pictures from his own memories for me to see. It didn't matter that my eighteen-year-old daughter was sitting right beside me, suddenly the year was 1978, and I was twelve years old again.

"I remember Estes Park and Big Thompson Pass," he said. "You kids threw snowballs at each other when we got to the Continental Divide. Do you remember that? And then you got sick—really sick. We had to find a clinic and get you to a doctor."

Dad talked about Pike's Peak, Grand Lake, and how, if he could, he would do the trip all over again. Then he told his daughter and granddaughter to enjoy every minute, to see as much as possible, and to drive safely. Before hanging up, he added that he loved us. I told him we loved him too, and then I thanked him for the walk down memory lane.

From that moment on, our day was wild and wonderful. Cote and I drove up Trail Ridge Road with vigor and vigilance, stopping at every lookout we could find. We hiked, we climbed, and we snapped tons of pictures. Not one, however, came close to capturing the true beauty before our eyes. I could try for days to describe the Rocky Mountains here on paper or provide a slew of photos inside this book, but both attempts would fall far short. These mountains must be seen firsthand, the crisp air inhaled through your own lungs, and the majesty of it all savored within your own soul.

Cote explored every inch of the mountain terrain we traveled, sometimes right out to what felt like the very edge. Together, we discovered hidden lakes and encountered hillside elk. We drove to the highest point (12,183 feet) and back down again, oohing and aahing at every turn. About halfway through one of our hikes, Cote suddenly stopped and stood perfectly still. As she gazed upon the vast Rocky Mountain horizon she exhaled, "This is amazing."

I couldn't help but think those same words myself as I watched her take it all in. We were right where we were supposed to be, and what an honor it was to be at my daughter's side. She was experiencing for the first time ever one of the most beautiful places on earth, and I was lucky enough to be her escort.

Cote and I played in the mountains until well past five o'clock that night. As we wound our way back down Trail Ridge Road, we stopped once to pick up a couple of carefully selected souvenirs: two huge rocks that had fallen from somewhere high above the cliff overhead. We heaved them onto the floorboards of our backseat and then continued onward, thrilled to have such one-of-a-kind mementos to keep with us forever.

From Trail Ridge Road we headed out across Highway 40 West, toward Steamboat Springs, Colorado. It was a long, winding and weary drive. By the time we pulled into town, Cote and I felt as if we had covered hundreds of miles, although according to our map, we barely budged an inch. Spending the day in the Rockies meant we would have a lot of ground to cover tomorrow, but that didn't bother me. I couldn't imagine doing anything differently today. The time I'd been given with my daughter was a precious gift—one that I knew could never be replaced.

Author's Note: If you have never been to Rocky Mountain National Forest, I recommend that you go. NOW. Don't put off a visit until that ever-elusive day known as Tomorrow. This is truly a must-see, bucket-list destination for all. Remember this one vital piece of information when you do go: there are absolutely no gas stations once you drive inside the forest.

How do I know?

Well, let's just say, Cote and I had barely enough fuel to get us from one end of Trail Ridge Road to the other. By the time we "fumed" our way into the one filling station located just outside the exit gate at Grand Lake, we both exhaled a sincere prayer of thanks and a huge sigh of relief.

Day 4: Steamboat Springs, Colorado to Battle Mountain, Nevada, 664 miles

You know, the Wise Men also traveled west.
~Peter T., email of encouragement, August 2009

I was awakened at two o'clock in the morning by the sound of typing. The clicking noise was clear and precise, even though I was completely submerged in a room full of darkness. For a moment, I couldn't remember where I was, but I did recall who I was with—and for the life of me, I couldn't understand why she would be texting at this ungodly hour.

"Are you texting?!"

"NO!"

"What are you doing?"

"Nothing!"

"Are you calling someone?"

"No!"

"Then why are you awake?"

"Because I'm looking at a map Daniel sent me."

"So you *are* on your computer."

"NO!"

"Cote, you're lying. How can you be looking at a map, if you're not on your computer?"

"What are you talking about?"

With that final outburst, a lightbulb flipped on inside my head. Cote was talking in her sleep. I was having a full-blown argument with my daughter, and she wasn't even somewhat awake.

I knew from experience that Cote was capable of holding entire conversations while submerged in the world of sleep, but never had I encountered an exchange like this one. Her answers were spot on, with her tone defiant and intense. Cote had even sprung straight up in bed and barked her first denial. For that reason, I thought for sure she was trying to hide some kind of electronic activity under the covers of darkness and blanket. Her answers kept pace with my questions, without a hint of hesitation. Yet through it all, she was totally and completely sound asleep.

Unfortunately, about the time I realized what was happening, Cote did too. The last thing she remembered from her dream-like state was her mother calling her a "liar"— which technically wasn't true. I said she was *lying*. I didn't say she was a *li-ar.* There can be a huge difference between those two words, unless it happens to be two o'clock in the morning, and you are on the receiving end of such a comment. Cote was ready for battle, her honor at stake. All I wanted to do was forget the whole fiasco and go back to sleep.

"I'm sorry I woke you up. Go back to sleep."

"No! You called me a liar."

"No, I didn't."

"Yes, you did."

"Cote, I heard a clicking noise, and I thought you were texting. But you weren't, you were sleeping. When you started talking to me in your sleep, I thought you were awake. But you weren't. Now it's over. Just go back to sleep."

"No! You called me a liar."

So begins Day 4…

Despite our riled emotions, the pull of sleep was too strong for either of us to fight. We both fell back asleep several minutes later.

However, I knew the incident was far from being over; it had only been postponed. Cote's defenses would surely rise up again with the rising of the sun. So when the first hint of morning light did crack through our curtain, I decided to get up and shower, letting Cote sleep a few extra minutes. I was hoping my actions would be seen as a peace offering, softening my daughter's stance and erasing some of our midnight madness.

I wasn't to be that lucky. When Cote crawled out from beneath her covers, I could tell she was still very much put out with me. We moved around our tiny motel room silently, closed off from each other. Given the nature of our fake argument, I did have to admit one thing—I definitely had some unresolved issues with the amount of time Cote was texting and spending on Facebook so far on our trip. If I had been honest with myself, I would have admitted she wasn't doing that much of either. Still, given my strong dislike of both, I found myself irritated by any attention Cote gave to these technological activities. Deep down, I knew I had to clear the air between us or else the next eight days were going to become unbearable. For the time being, however, pure stubbornness blocked any form of reconciliation.

I'll say one thing for small motel rooms: there's no place to hide. Vying for both bathroom and repacking space, Cote and I kept coming face-to-face, while our bodies skimmed past each other, rigid and cold. We exchanged knowing glances, yet we remained mute and trapped within ourselves. It took finally sitting down on the beds across from each other, leaning over to tie our shoes, for our eyes to lock and our guards to fall.

I told Cote I was sorry for jumping to conclusions, and she graciously accepted my apology.

Although I still had no idea what it was that I heard during the night, she understood how her reaction had thrown me on the defensive. I ventured further and opened up as to how I felt about her texting. To her credit, she gave pause to see things from her mother's point of view. Finally, we hugged, squeezing the remaining hurt of our piercing words away.

By the time Cote and I checked out of our motel, we were at ease with each other and ourselves once again. We were ready to hit the road and put some miles behind us. We left Steamboat Springs at 9:00 a.m., Mountain Time, and logged almost seven hundred miles before the day was through.

We resisted the temptation to reunite with fast-moving I-80, and stayed instead on the lonely, quiet stretch of Highway 40. This back road had very little to offer in terms of scenery, except for a few red foothills and a couple of very small towns, but the slower pace was a welcome change. The miles slipped by, with us rarely meeting another wayfaring traveler.

We passed through Hayden and Maybell, Elk Springs and Dinosaur (yes, that's right.) All were itty-bitty blips on the map that hardly registered an arrival or departure to those passing through. Cote and I stopped only once out there in the middle of nowhere.

At a lonely convenience store, we purchased a stick of beef jerky and a frozen Snickers ice cream bar. We thought the clerk would be delighted to see us, welcoming some lighthearted conversation to help pass her day. We couldn't have been more wrong. As we approached the counter, she kept her eyes lowered and rang up our order with barely an audible, "Thank you." There was no indication she'd like us to linger, so Cote and I quickly left the store and climbed back into our waiting car.

Around one o'clock in the afternoon, civilization reappeared as we neared Park City, Utah. I remembered visiting this quaint storybook town several years ago, enjoying its unique shops and one-of-a-kind boutiques. I decided at the very last minute to take the exit and show the mountainside village to Cote. We could afford an hour of browsing, and it would do us good to stretch our legs and get some fresh air.

Pulling into town, we lucked out and snagged one of the few available parallel parking spots. Feeling euphoric over our good fortune, we opened our car doors, only to be slammed with 104-degree heat. Our air-conditioned bodies were thrown into a state of shock. This was definitely not the kind of fresh air I had in mind.

Despite the crushing temperatures, Cote and I still wanted to take a quick look around town, so we closed our car doors and started down the block. Within minutes, we both knew we weren't interested in actually shopping. The upscale stores reeked of excessive materialism, contradicting the simplicity of the journey we were on. Cote's rite of passage had always been about getting to the heart of things, not about letting things get the better of our wallet.

Nevertheless, one particular shop caught our attention, a Native American art and jewelry store. Through the open doorway, we could see a dark, cool, inviting interior. Cote and I entered and were immediately drawn farther inside by one stunning piece of artwork after another. Eventually, we reached the back of the store, where an older gray-haired gentleman stood oddly silent behind the sales counter. Cote and I instinctively offered easy smiles as a way of introduction, but to our surprise, his stoic face didn't flinch. He uttered not a word.

Puzzled, *(Isn't he happy to have a customer or two come through the door? No one is here except for us.)*, Cote and I continued to browse the first-floor of his art-filled establishment. It didn't take long for us to realize why his welcome had been so meager, so miserly. The bracelet sparkling up at me through the spotless glass showcase had a price tag of $400. The hand-painted and signed picture Cote was eyeing listed for $2,500. The topper was the skillfully woven rug hanging from the banister leading to the second floor, which taunted a price tag of $5,000, and held an additional warning to any admirer passing by: *DO NOT TOUCH.*

Now we knew exactly why the shopkeeper had been so uninviting, and I'll admit he was right. Cote and I were not potential customers. He'd been in this business, in this up-scale town, long enough to recognize buyers verses browsers. True, Cote and I wouldn't be spending money in his store, but we didn't deserve his rude behavior, either.

Secretly, my daughter and I made eye contact and raised knowing eyebrows. Without whispering a word, we both knew what to do. We would verbally become the patrons he was accustomed to. Cote and I started by going gooey over how beautiful the woven rug was and how absolutely striking it would look in our den back home. We pointed to the signed and framed landscape and commented how it would be perfect above the buffet in our dining room. We moseyed upstairs, fingering trinkets left and right, interjecting comments here and there. When we finally reached the top landing, out of sight from our boorish host below, we turned to each other with faces plastered in total disbelief. *How rude is he? How pompous?*

Yes, we were dressed in T-shirts and cargo shorts. And no, we weren't going to buy anything in his precious, expensive store. But did that give him the right to be so cold and uninviting?

Cote and I were just beginning to spew our frustrations when we heard footsteps climbing the stairs beneath us. *What in the world??!! Are you kidding me??!!*

Sure enough, the owner was coming upstairs. When he reached the second floor, he crossed his arms, and stood before us in continued silence. He didn't have to say a word; his message was loud and clear. *Please leave.* So we did. But on our own terms, taking our sweet ol' time.

Cote and I exchanged more pleasantries and turned over more one-of-a-kind keepsakes, while we casually headed back downstairs and leisurely drifted out the door. Once we hit the sidewalk, we let our feelings fly. Cote and I tore this guy's demeanor apart limb by limb. We unleashed the anger bottled up inside and stomped across the street to *Cows*, a highly regarded ice cream shop. There's nothing like some frozen dairy to cool down a couple of hot-tempered women.

Thankfully, the salesgirl behind the parlor counter was as sweet as the treat she scooped up for us. She even took the time to compliment Cote on her fork bracelet*, pointing out its unique design and appreciating Cote's creativity in crafting it. We told her she could make one for herself for the cost of about a dollar, which was much better than the prices being charged for the jewelry across the street. We thanked her for her hospitality, collected our cones, and made a beeline for the car. Within minutes, Cote and I closed the cover on this "storybook" town. We had read enough and were glad to be putting this chapter behind us.

From Park City, we drove straight-through Salt Lake City

without a single desire to stop. The expressway was crazy, the traffic intense. Taking an exit would only have added to the stress. The mountains, however, were gorgeous in the full afternoon sun. I couldn't tear my eyes away from them even when all that was left was their reflection in my rearview mirror.

As the city faded, Cote and I began to take notice of a strange white substance collecting along the highway. *"What is it?"* we wondered, never for a moment thinking the obvious. As we drove mile after mile, the white stuff inched farther and farther out from the shoulder of the road. Eventually, it spread as far as we could see. The flat, drab terrain was nothing but a sheet of white. That's when it finally hit us.

Of course! Salt! Cote and I laughed at our lack of common sense, but growing up in the Midwest, we had never seen anything like this before. The entire Great Salt Desert of Utah was upon us; everything had turned to milky-white. There was not a green tree, bush, or blade of grass anywhere to be found.

Soon Cote and I were more than just amused by the expansive fields of salt. As our trek continued towards the Nevada border, we became intrigued. *What does it feel like? Is it hard and compact? Or loose like sand on a beach? If we walk on it, will our toes wiggle in or will our soles flinch, as if on gravel?* Finally, with only twenty miles left to go before we crossed the state line, I turned to Cote and said, "Let's pull over the next chance we get and see what this stuff's like for real."

Right then a rest stop came into view. I flipped on my blinker and pulled the car into the paved parking lot. As we approached the pavilion, we saw the sign stating our whereabouts: The Bonneville Salt Flats, home of the world-famous land-speed record runs.

Others were there too, milling around, checking out the phenomenon. The scene was amazing. Coarse, dense salt was everywhere the eye could see. Cote and I wandered away from the crowd and walked across the flat, hard-packed surface. The first thing we decided to do was taste it, so we found an untouched spot to pinch a few grains off the top layer. Our tongues curled on contact. The flavor was so intense, so sharp. Next, we took off our shoes and walked gingerly upon the vast sea of white, feeling the roughness of the surface poke sharply at the bottoms of our feet. Finally, we tried to scoop up some grains to bring home, but that proved easier said than done. After several futile attempts by hand, I finally retrieved the metal cup from our thermos back in the car to scrape the top layer loose. Cote and I snapped some silly pictures, we wrote our names with a few found rocks, then washed the salt from our feet and headed back to the open highway.

It was now very late in the afternoon, and we still had more than two hundred miles to go. Thank goodness for another time zone change, as we were able to "add" an extra hour to our day. By nightfall, we drove into the town of Battle Mountain, Nevada, about halfway across the state.

It was only Wednesday, and crazy to think we'd left home just four short days ago. Here we were, almost all the way across the country. I was getting excited about seeing the Pacific coast, but also growing nervous about climbing the trees. After spending yesterday in the Rockies, I realized how nerve-wracking it was to watch Cote lean over a guardrail or step to the very edge of a look-out point. If that made me nervous, then how anxious was I going to be when she climbed two hundred feet up in the air, strapped only to a rope and suspended from a single branch high overhead?

Our dream of climbing trees was quickly drawing closer. Come Saturday we would face the Douglas fir we'd traveled so far to scale. I knew tonight was not the time to start questioning Cote's rite of passage. We were in too deep, and the pinnacle of our journey—sitting and sleeping in the canopy of a very tall tree—was just days away. Nevertheless, the microscopic seeds of doubt were now sprouting in the corners of my mind.

Am I really being a good parent in all of this? Or am I allowing my daughter to take a risk that will prove to be too great? Is this adventure truly about learning to live fully in the given moments of everyday life, or am I being naïve and foolish as to what we are really doing out here?

So many questions; no real answers. As I turned out the light on Day 4, I said a prayer that God would ease my fears and give me the courage to face the morning—which in faith I knew would be like any other new day—full of unknowns and what ifs.

*Cote's fork bracelet is literally a *fork* bracelet. Her dad fashioned it for her one day, by bending a typical dinner fork around her wrist. She now wears it daily, along with several other braided and beaded bracelets, and the combined effect definitely complements her style and personality.

Author's Note: The clicking sound that awakened me on Day 4 was actually Cote grinding her teeth in her sleep. The mystery was solved several nights later when, unfortunately, she did it again.

Day 5: Battle Mountain, Nevada to Crescent City, California, 545 miles

Take what you've learned so far and broaden it. Be a good listener. Be a good friend.
But don't let people use you. Don't forget where you came from and who you are.
And remember, we all love you very much.

~Aunt Sis, Rite of Passage letter, August 2009

Cote and I drove from Nevada to Oregon and into California today. Three states with unique features and graceful beauty.

We left Battle Mountain early in the morning and turned north on Highway 95, leaving all traces of civilization behind us. Sagebrush and long stretches of rocky desert became our only companions as we crossed terrain so desolate Cote's cell phone lost all reception. Road signs became our form of entertainment and our only link to the outside world.

We read warnings from Smokey the Bear about fire safety and saw other signs preparing us for unexpected wild donkey crossings. Farther down the road, a huge black-and-white signpost informed us it was our duty to report any highway shootings we may witness; it gave a 1-800 number to call. There were signs advising us against falling rock, snow zones, steep downgrades, and soft shoulders. There were no farms, no homes, no other items of interest to gaze upon. We were just a mother and daughter on a journey, looking for signs.

Way out in the middle of no-man's land, we turned off Highway

95 and onto Route 140 west. This road would lead us to the Oregon border, but we still had well over one hundred miles to travel before we'd get there. Occasionally, a huge mountain rose up from the dry, dusty ground, and we'd have to steer our car up one side and back down the other as the narrow two-lane road curved precariously at times.

Finally, Oregon arrived, and with it came a few farms, a few cattle, and a few fields. Not many to start with—just one here, and then several miles later, another one there. These distractions were enough, though, to break up the mind-numbing nothingness of our route and boost our spirits. Little did we know, however, that Oregon had something else in store for us, as well.

Less than an hour into this state, while still driving through a particularly barren stretch of land, a wicked storm blew in. This one made our Nebraska squall seem like a run-of-the-mill summer shower. Within minutes, our car was engulfed in a sheet of rain so dense that we couldn't see through the windshield, even with the wipers set at maximum speed. A solid gray curtain of water dropped from the heavens above, surrounding our vehicle on every side, closing us off from the rest of the world. There was absolutely no place to run, no place to hide, nothing we could do.

Just when I thought the storm couldn't get any worse, it did. The rain turned to hail. I couldn't believe my eyes or my ears. Hard-packed, dime-sized ice chips pelted our car's roof and hood. The sound was both deafening and sickening. All I could think about were thousands of tiny pockmarks scarring the black paint of our baby-faced, five-month-old Ford Edge. I pulled over to the side of the road, hoping against hope that by sitting still the assault would be less severe. Tears began to sting my eyes, but when Cote saw me start to crumble, she would have no part of it. In a crazy *Freaky Friday* kind of moment, she took on the role of adult, while her mother sat curled up and sniveling like a baby in the driver's seat.

"Mom, it's okay. Its just a car. It can be fixed. There's nothing we can do about it, so just let it go. Everything will be all right."

I wanted so badly to believe her, like a child does when soothed by a parent's tender voice. I stopped my whimpering, but squeezed my eyes shut as the hail continued to pelt us. And then I heard the shutter click on Cote's camera. Once again, she was capturing our moments on film.

The storm finally passed, and as the last few drops of rain hit our windshield, I slowly reopened my eyes. I felt like Dorothy waking up in the world of Oz. Everything around us was vibrant with new color. Rolling down my window, I breathed in air that was fresh and bursting clean. The dry, brittle, dust-covered wrapper that had encased us for the past two days had been stripped off and tossed aside. After Cote and I checked the exterior of the car, which was miraculously mark-free, we climbed back in and I put the car in gear. With renewed excitement, we pressed on.

The color green bled into every nook and cranny of Oregon the farther we drove into the state. Everything came alive around us. We drove through fields of grass and groves of pine. Yes! We finally had trees—beautiful, green, soul-pleasing trees! They grew small at first, miniature-like, but inched taller and wider the farther we made our way towards the waiting ocean.

As the trees gradually increased in size, Cote and I felt a sense of renewed hope growing inside us too. We had weathered a storm to get here. It had been dark and scary and upsetting. Yet, on every journey through life, how often is this the path one has to follow? Sometimes it takes getting through the bad times in order to recognize and appreciate the good ones when they arrive.

More miles passed. California continued to draw closer. We were now sandwiched by trees on either side; we were burrowed between their outstretched limbs. Cote and I settled into our drive, allowing the feeling of safety and security coming from this green stretch of highway to relax us. The air now held a hint of ocean, drifting in through the car's dashboard vents. The salty breeze was faint, but rising—tickling our noses, teasing our senses, adding to our anticipation of reaching the Pacific coast.

Dusk had fallen by the time we crossed the California border. According to our map, we had only about fifty miles to go before we reached Crescent City, but Highway 199 was full of twists, turns, and razor-sharp curves. A foggy mist turned into a light drizzly rain with the setting of the evening sun, making our drive painstakingly slow as we used caution on the unfamiliar roads. Cote and I knew we were close to our destination, yet every mile we logged seemed like ten. We were exhausted, but still filled with excitement, anxious to reach the coast and let our eyes fall finally upon the Pacific.

Highway 199 ended at Route 101, which led us into Crescent City. The fog still loomed large throughout the town, shielding the ocean from view, but we were thankful to be here and quickly pulled our car into the parking lot of the first motel we could find. I walked in, approached the front desk, and asked for a room.

The night clerk told me they were booked solid.

What? No! We've come so far! We're finally here! There has to be a room!

Nervous, I returned to the car and asked Cote to start praying.

She had Hannah on the phone, so she enlisted her sister to do the same. The clerk inside had told me our only hope for a room tonight would be the Hampton Inn down the road, which I could see through the fog and light rain. It was a grandiose hotel perched right out on the water's edge, the one with the coveted ocean view. *The rooms there surely have to cost a fortune,* I thought.

However, this was a special occasion. Cote and I had driven over 2,300 miles to get here; we were on her once-in-a-lifetime rite of passage. Up to this point, we had spent very little on lodging, and by looking at this place I knew the nightly rate would be well worth it. As I walked inside, I readied myself to pay full price—if I had to.

Back in Steamboat Springs, Colorado, I had stumbled upon a business practice I never knew before—the rates for hotel rooms could be negotiated. *If,* that is, the one seeking to book a room is bold enough to initiate the bartering process. Cote and I had been successful back in Steamboat, even when the hotel where we stopped was the only place left with rooms for rent. When I asked the night clerk back in Colorado if that was the best price he had to offer, he immediately agreed to lower the rate by twenty-five dollars. I about fell over at my good luck. I figured my chances here in Crescent City would be a bit slimmer, but it still couldn't hurt to ask.

I made my way up to the long, lean counter at the Hampton Inn, where I was greeted by an older gentleman, wearing both an air of importance and a freshly pressed uniform. *The manager,* was my first thought. Further down the check-in counter stood a much younger- looking "manager-wannabe" type, who was busy helping another couple book a room.

"Good evening. May I help you?" the elder gentleman asked.

"Yes. Do you have any rooms available tonight?"

"Only a few left, but let me see. We do have one on the third floor, with a balcony overlooking the ocean."

"Uh, huh. And how much does that one run?"

"Well, our regular rate would be..." He wrote the figure on a small piece of paper and slid it over for me to read. *$259!* My heart lurched up to my throat, but I swallowed hard and did my best to hold my composure. As this number took its time digesting on the inside, I hoped it only looked like I was weighing my options on the outside. In my shock-induced pause, the manager misread my silence for actual contemplation, and quickly rushed on.

"But I can discount it for you tonight, and let you have it for..."

Again he scribbled. This time the note read $159. Much better, of course, but my mind was now racing. *Why is he being so discrete? Am I supposed to counteroffer? Will he be shocked if I do?*

I smiled, and then in an attempt at stalling a bit longer, I inquired about the hotel's amenities.

"A full hot continental breakfast, of course. Use of all the facilities. Free wi-fi."

I did my best to look pleased, while still trying to give a slight hint of uncertainty.

"I see. Hmmm...You know, my daughter and I just drove all the way from Michigan to get here to the Pacific coast. It's been a really long trip. You don't, by chance, have a special rate for Michigan guests, do you?"

Then I smiled as sweet and sincerely as my tired, dusty face could muster.

"Well, I suppose for our guests from Michigan, I could let you have it for..."

Scribble, scribble...$139!

Jumping for joy on the inside, I accepted his offer calmly on the outside. Yes, it was only another twenty-dollar discount, but when all was said and done, we had just snagged a $259 room overlooking the Pacific Ocean in a town almost fully-booked, for only $139. I was ecstatic, a tad bit proud, and ready to go fetch Cote. We had just found a room at the Inn.

Unfortunately, night had now fully fallen, with no break from the fog. We'd have to wait until morning to see the ocean from our balcony, but that was all right with us tonight. By the time Cote and I dropped our backpacks, we were ready to wash up and call it a day.

Twenty minutes later, I returned to the car for a couple of items we forgot to bring in.

Passing through the lobby, I overheard the young hotel clerk apologizing to a new arrival, explaining that the Hampton Inn was completely booked for the night. So, it was true. We did get one of the very last rooms available. Our prayers had been heard and answered. Though I felt sorry for the too-late traveler, after stepping outside into the cool night air, I couldn't help but look up and say a silent word of thanks for our good fortune.

Cote and I had been led to this perfect spot. Come morning, we'd open our eyes to an ocean wide and blue. Hand in hand, we would walk upon its shoreline, glancing back to see how far we'd come and looking forward to all that was yet to be.

Day 6: Crescent City, California, Morning on the Coast

Twenty years from now you will be more disappointed by the things that you didn't do than by the ones you did do. So throw off the bowlines. Sail away from the safe harbor. Catch the trade winds in your sails. Explore. Dream. Discover.

-Mark Twain

I woke up early this morning, way before daylight. By nature, I'm not one to fall back asleep once my eyes flutter open, but I knew there wasn't even the slightest chance of doing that today. Waiting outside our hotel door were two of the world's greatest wonders— the mighty Pacific Ocean and the towering California Redwoods— and we had only one day to see them both. By nightfall, Cote and I needed to be in Eugene, Oregon, preparing for our long-awaited tree climb. With just twelve short hours on the clock, I knew I wanted to start moving as early as possible.

I slipped from beneath my covers and padded my way softly to the balcony. As I slid open the thin glass door, the sound of the ocean washed over me, delighting my ears like beautifully orchestrated music. The world outside was still pitch-black, so I couldn't see the water, but I could feel it. Soon the filtering rays of morning would rise up and bring the panoramic view to full light.

I knew where I needed to be when that happened—standing at the water's edge. The Pacific was pulling on me as surely as the moon pulls on the ocean's tide. It would have been easy to let Cote sleep, to let her stay inside the warmth of her dreams. I could have quietly slipped out of the room, and explored the coast in solitude, murmuring my morning prayers. That was a ritual I daily exercised back home, and I knew Cote wouldn't question my actions had I chosen to do this today. My heart, though, knew differently. Walking out without waking her up, asking if she wanted to come with me, was completely unthinkable. I stepped back inside the room, leaned over her blanketed body, and shook her gently.

"Cote."

"Huh?"

"Cote, it's morning. It's early, really early, but I'm going to go down to the water. Do you want to come with me?"

"What? What time is it?"

"Not yet six o'clock. But I want to be down there before the sun comes up. You don't have to go, but I didn't want to leave without asking you."

"No. I think I'll stay here. Is that alright?"

"Yeah, that's fine. It's just that we've come all this way, and we're finally here. I want to be out there on the water when the sun comes up. I don't want to miss it."

A heavy sigh escaped from somewhere deep beneath the blanket.

"Hold on. I'm coming with you."

We didn't waste time with makeup or hairstyles. We simply brushed our teeth and slipped on our sandals. Dressed in our comfy pajama pants and sweatshirts, we headed downstairs and crossed the lobby, where I spotted several thermoses of hot coffee. I grabbed a quick cup to go, and then Cote and I stepped outside into the cool morning air.

The first hints of daylight were just beginning to tinge the eastern sky. We climbed over the grassy embankment and gingerly picked our way across pebbles and driftwood to the water's edge. Without saying a word, we both knew what we were going to do first.

Standing side by side, we dipped our toes into the blue Pacific Ocean. The chilly water sent shock waves up our legs, but we kept our feet submerged, watching as the gentle waves skirted around our ankles. Multicolored rocks sparkled up at us through the crystal-clear water, each one a tiny precious gemstone. We were here—really here. We had driven as far west as the open road would take us. Nothing about the journey felt over for me, though. In fact, the world felt only new and full of possibility. As with everything in life, it's how you choose to look at things. For me, today wasn't an ending. It was a new beginning waiting to happen.

Cote and I stood there together for several silent minutes, watching as the sun slowly pushed the dark of night away, lighting the sky to a soft shade of gray. Huge, slick boulders materialized from the shadows, rising from the ocean like giant sea creatures. The rocky coastline was gorgeous and growing wider as the sun continued to spread its rays. Then the most amazing thing happened—the rocks began to move!

What? How? In disbelief, we squinted and pointed, confused by the boulders wiggling to life.

"Over there!" Cote exclaimed. "Did you see that?"

Finally, the sun's rays rose high enough to erase the last traces of night from our coastline. Into full view came harbor seals—thirty or more of them, right before our very eyes. They stretched and yawned, groaned and grunted. They had been there the whole time, sleeping as the world slept. Now they were awakening and welcoming the new light of day right along with us.

Cote and I stood silent and awestruck. What an incredible sight to witness. These impressive animals came to life, bold and beautiful, and we were transfixed by their transformation. It was difficult to take our eyes off of them, but knowing there was much more here for us to explore, Cote and I finally had to turn our attention down the beach and begin walking.

Scavenging the shoreline for the most unusual stones, we filled my now empty coffee cup with our newly found treasures. We drifted in between and around some of the closer rock formations, climbing a few and sliding our fingers across their slippery surfaces. We even peeked inside the cracks and crevices so we didn't miss a thing.

Farther down the coast, we met and talked with a local woman out walking her dog. Soon after, we happened upon a few fishermen wading in thigh-high water, poking poles under several massive boulders. Having no clue what they were fishing for, Cote and I stopped to watch. When they failed to pull anything from the water, we finally called out to them. "What are you hoping to catch?"

"Eels," they replied, explaining that the snakelike creatures hide beneath the rocks when the tide goes back out to sea. "They make good eating," one young fisherman claimed.

We watched a while longer, exchanged a few more questions and answers, then Cote and I moved on down the shoreline.

Eventually we wound our way back to where we started, the beach in front of our hotel. Something here had caught our eye when we first climbed over the grassy embankment and we wanted to get a closer look.

A stick shelter had been constructed from large pieces of

driftwood. The size of it was impressive, almost like a small wooden hut. When we first arrived at daybreak, two young people—a guy and a girl—seemed to be its owners. They had been sitting on the pebbly shoreline close to the structure, but not exactly close to each other. They appeared rumpled and somewhat removed, but now they were gone. Cote and I ventured closer to the driftwood shelter, circled around it, and then stepped inside.

Someone has spent the night here.

There was a small makeshift fire pit smoldering with fresh ashes, and a fast-food wrapper wadded up into a ball in the corner. Two log stools were pushed back against the far wall, making just enough open space to spread out a sleeping bag. Maybe the young couple we had seen earlier had done just that—spent the night here. Maybe they were far from home, like Cote and me, but not lucky enough to have found a room. Or, perhaps, they were a couple local teenagers who had snuck out for the night. Maybe they were two kids seeking adventure, or possibly two lost souls, homeless and adrift. We didn't know their story, but while Cote and I poked around, we continued to write and rewrite their blank, unknown pages inside our minds.

After a full hour of exploring, talking, climbing and collecting rocks, hunger finally overtook us. Cote and I made our way back inside the hotel to grab a bite to eat. Sitting down in front of the huge plate-glass window, offering a spectacular view of the ocean, we ate our breakfast of eggs, toast, and sausage.

About the time we were finishing up, Cote and I saw the rumpled young man return, wandering back towards the hotel from down the rocky shoreline. He was alone, his head bent low. He seemed to be studying the ground he walked upon, careful where he placed his next step. As he drew closer to the stick shelter, Cote expressed an interest in him. She was curious to know where he was from, what had brought him here, and where he might be going.

"Go talk to him," I said.

"What? No way. I couldn't do that. What would I say?"

"I don't know. Just walk out there. See what happens."

"Uh, uh. What if he thinks I'm weird? Or what if the girl shows up and thinks I'm hitting on him?"

"So what? You're not. Besides, you're in a safe place, Cote. You're in front of a hotel full of people. I'll be sitting right here if you need anything. Go out there and see what happens. Say something if it feels right. If it doesn't, just sit there and look at the ocean. If you don't at least try, you'll always wonder what might have happened if you did. Think about it...what do you have to lose? And what might you have to gain?"

To my amazement, Cote wiped her hands, stood up, and said she would do it. Now it was up to me to sit still and watch, as she walked out the door, climbed over the embankment, and took the trail leading down to the water. I was both nervous and proud. She wouldn't be holding my hand, nor would she have her mother along acting as a buffer to any possible embarrassment that may come her way. She had only herself to fall back on. I silently prayed that if needed, she would uncover a strength inside herself—one that had been there all along, but was just waiting to be called up and put to use.

After Cote left, I opened my journal and began to make a few sketches. I needed to distract myself from the fact that my eldest child was now out of sight and out in the world without me. I forced myself to give her time, and I forced myself to trust that this was the right thing to do. I had to let her go, if only just this little bit. I took a deep breath and imagined myself superglued to the chair beneath me. Though anxious to learn what was happening, I fought the urge inside me to run out after her.

At the twenty-minute mark, I gathered my things, refilled my coffee cup and went to go find her. I figured that was enough time for her to make something happen, and it was all the time my nerves could handle. I found Cote sitting quietly on a large piece of driftwood, all alone, and lost in thought. The rumpled girl had returned, and she was farther down the shore with rumpled boy. Once again, they were close to the shelter, but still not really near each other. I went and sat next to my daughter, curious about what had, or had not, happened.

"I didn't talk to him."

"No? Why not?"

"Well, I waited for a bit and just kind of watched to see if he might look up so I could say something. But he kept his head down, and then the girl came back. I thought about going up to the two of them, but it just didn't feel right. So I came over here and sat down instead."

"That's okay, Cote. You followed your gut, and that's a good thing. You gave it a shot, so no regrets, right? I gotta tell ya, that's a whole lot more than what most people would have done."

"Yeah, maybe. It's just that I would still like to know their story, you know? I bet they have a lot of stuff going on."

"Yeah, I bet you're right. I bet they do."

We sat there a while longer, not wanting to leave the ebb and flow of either the ocean or our own private thoughts. We soaked up the remaining magical moments of the morning—silently reviewing our gifts of discovery and truth. When the time felt right, Cote and I stood and headed back to our room to get ready for the rest of our day. We had a grove of towering trees waiting for us down the road. The ocean had given us an opportunity to look out and look within. The redwoods, with their sacred branches stretching high overhead, would draw our eyes towards the very heavens above.

I couldn't even begin to imagine what discoveries were waiting for us there.

Day 6: Crescent City, California, After-noon in the Redwoods

The redwoods, once seen, leave a mark or create a vision
that stays with you always.
No one has ever successfully painted or photographed a
redwood tree.
The feeling they produce is not transferable. From them
comes silence and awe.
~John Steinbeck, *Travels with Charley*

Cote and I took Hwy 101 north, backtracking a bit, to reach the Redwoods National Forest. We had driven this exact same stretch of highway just the night before, but the evening fog, the drizzle, and our own state of exhaustion, had hidden all the overwhelming beauty before us now.

Everything was large, green, and alive in the bright, warm sunshine. With our good night's sleep and our morning walk, our spirits felt refreshed and our energy levels high. The trees lining the roadside were growing bigger and taller with each passing mile. As Cote and I approached the entrance to the national park, she couldn't help but laugh at me every time I craned my neck to see through the top two inches of our windshield. I was trying with all that I had to take in the full height of these beautiful redwoods.

"Mom, would you just look up through the sunroof and stop being such a goof."

"Oh, yeah. I guess I could do that."

But within seconds, I would be overtaken again by the sheer size of yet another glorious giant, and I would find myself pressed to the steering wheel, my eyes straining upward, my mouth gaping open.

We really didn't know what to expect when we arrived inside the Redwood National Forest, and without a map to guide us, Cote and I didn't know where to go. So we simply drove slowly, gawking in every given direction, but mostly up. There were little dirt side roads forking off the wide, well-maintained one we were driving, each seeming to lead to hidden places deep within the forest glades. We finally turned left, leaving the main route behind, having no idea where we were headed, but excited and eager to find out.

The side road quickly narrowed, squeezing us between rows of redwoods, ferns, and foliage. Little pull-offs were available in case two cars met up, but so far that didn't seem to be a problem. We were all alone on this trail, nestled safe inside the warm, inviting, outstretched arms of the towering trees.

Being caged inside the car, however, started to drive us crazy. Cote and I needed to break loose; we had to touch and inspect these beauties close up. Another little pull-over presented itself, so I maneuvered the car to the side of the road. Pushing our doors open, the rich, forest air burst through our noses, filling our lungs with its strong, pungent smell. We stopped short, breathed deep, and felt ourselves absorb, pore by pore, this brand-new world we were stepping into.

With the car's motor turned off, the forest became a hushed and holy chapel. When we spoke, our voices echoed back to us from the canopies far overhead. Cote and I began to explore, finding hidden nooks and crannies in the trunks of trees growing so close to each other that they appeared to be attached. We climbed up between their bases, using bark-covered ledges to balance and hold ourselves. We circled around several particularly wide trees, letting their coarse woody exteriors scrape against our trailing palms, leaving temporary imprints upon our hands and lasting impressions upon our hearts.

Our exploring led us to the other side of the one-lane road, where we discovered the four-foot-high stump of a mighty redwood long since gone. It took some effort to hoist ourselves up to the top of the cut surface, but once we did, Cote and I stood frozen in utter disbelief. The diameter of the trunk that stretched out beneath our feet was incredible. We could walk across it, lie down upon it, and lower ourselves into the deep crevice that years of decay had carved into the redwood's core. At first it felt as if we were playing on a mini-playground. We swirled and spun, like dancers on a stage. Then in one sobering thought, the wooden platform became something far more meaningful—something sacred and divine.

Cote and I stopped our fun and imagined the tree that once stood here. Despite the thousands of others still growing strong around us, we somehow felt the painful loss of this single solitary giant. We sat down quietly and traced the trunk's inner rings with our fingertips, sliding our touch across the names carved into the hallowed bands. Many people had been here before us, leaving their mark behind. For a minute, Cote and I considered adding our own names, carving a permanent record of her rite of passage—*August 2009*.

"Do you want to carve your name, Cote?"

"I don't know. Do you?"

"I don't know." Silence settled over us for a brief moment, as we considered the possibility, then I added, "There's a part of me that does, but I think there's a bigger part of me that doesn't. In a way, it doesn't feel right."

"I know. It seems so disrespectful."

Our conversation turned into a deeper discussion about the environment and the role we both play in caring for it. We talked about how our perspectives and actions affect the world we live in, either directly or indirectly. As we shared our thoughts, the engraved names in front of us became even more arrogant and out of place. Adding our own would be like adding insult to injury— sprinkling salt, if you will, upon an open wound. We couldn't do it. We wouldn't do it. Instead, we stood up and left this place exactly as we had found it.

From this private two-person sanctuary, we headed down the road towards Stout Memorial Grove, a well-visited section of the Jedediah Smith Redwoods State Park. This time we parked our car next to several others and hiked a short distance to the infamous stand of trees, our eyes taking in every inch of the magnificent forest. This was truly nature's wooded wonderland, intentionally protected and carefully preserved.

We could dance around, climb up, crawl over, tuck in, and hide behind, tree after gigantic tree. The grove was nothing but redwoods, stoic and strong, solid soldiers standing at full attention. The ones that had fallen were huge and impressive too, and in their decaying state still served a great and noble purpose—to generously feed the roots of those still growing around them. The living trees were very much dependent upon the nourishment of the dying ones.

It was here that I gave Cote her next letter, which was tucked inside a very special box. Both were a gift from her sister, Hannah. As Cote sat in the crook of a tree and opened her treasure, I stepped back to give her space. I didn't want to either crowd or interfere. This was her personal moment, her private message. Cote read the note and savored the words. When she finished, she slipped the letter back inside the box and then came to rejoin me.

We spent the rest of the day playing inside this grand grove of towering trees. I watched as Cote moved about, lithe and cat-like, much like Mowgli in the movie *The Jungle Book*. She was a natural, her actions based on instinct. The girl skipped and jumped and performed ballet. At times, she even seemed to defy gravity. Cote pushed herself in her game of exploration but at one point, I had to stop and ask her to rethink what she was about to do.

Having climbed upon the cut end of a huge fallen redwood, she wanted to take to a running leap to the other side, jumping across the space where a section of a tree trunk had been removed to clear the trail.

"Cote, wait a minute. Are you sure you want to do this?"

"Yes. And I want you to take my picture when I do."

"Excuse me, but that means I'd have to watch, and I'm not sure I can."

"C'mon, Mom. Tell me when you're ready."

I snapped the picture, the frame catching my daughter in midair. It was a great action shot—Cote barefoot, with the suggestion of invisible wings upon her shoulders. She made the jump, but just by the skin of her knees. She caught the other side waist-high and pulled herself up the rest of the way. Expelling my breath, I was relieved it was over.

"Should I jump back?"

"Excuse me? No!"

"Why not?"

" Ah, let's see…maybe because you barely made it the first time."

"But, I did make it. And now I wanna try and jump back."

"Cote, let's think about this for a minute, okay? You made the jump the first time. You proved that you could do it. If you jump back now, you'll be landing on the narrower part of the trunk, and the side that's smoother. All this means there's a higher risk you're gonna fall."

"But life is about taking risks, remember? 'Fully participating everyday' and all that."

"Okay, what I mean when I say that is, life does involve intentionally taking risks, *sometimes*. Good risks, Cote. Carefully, thought-out ones. Risks that make living more meaningful. Not about taking *every* risk that comes along. Think about it. Tomorrow you're supposed to climb a tree. A very big tree—huge! One that grows over two-hundred-fifty feet into the air. You've waited a longtime to do this. Over a year. What if you jump right now, on a whim, and then fall and break your leg? You won't be able to climb tomorrow's tree. You won't be able to make this bigger dream of yours come true. So is it worth the risk to jump again right now, when you know it may cost you climbing the tree tomorrow?"

Despite my impeccably sound argument, it still took my daughter several minutes to agree and climb down. This scenario was a life lesson, however. Hopefully, Cote would someday look back and realize I wasn't just being an overprotective mother this afternoon. Jumping back was truly not a risk worth taking; its price tag was just too high to pay.

Leaving the massive tree trunk behind, we turned to hike deeper into the national forest. As if cast under a spell, the redwoods pulled us in, begging us to inspect and explore them. One in particular caught Cote's attention, and she stopped to study it from every standing angle, top to bottom. Then she did something that threw me completely off-guard. Cote dropped to the ground and stretched out flat on her back right beneath the colossal tree. She wanted to see what it would look like from a laying down point of view. It didn't matter that pine needles were collecting in her hair or that people passing by would think she was crazy. Cote was conducting an important experiment; she was capturing this tree from a whole new perspective. Looking at her lying there, I knew I wanted to experience it too.

Side by side, pine needles poking our backsides, we gazed up into the redwood's vast green canopy. There was something calming about this position. Our breathing slowed, as we entered a higher realm of consciousness. Our eyes settled on the shafts of sunlight filtering and dancing between the branches, casting white-gold streaks upon the leaves and our faces. We could feel the solidness of the earth, the roots beneath the soil woven tightly together. We were grounded, yet the view had us floating featherlight. The moment was incredible. Cote snapped a few pictures, including one where we joined our hands together in the shape of a heart, recording our love for this tree, this place. We were a mother and daughter, taking on the world, lying down.

It was late afternoon when Cote and I returned to our car. As much as we hated to leave the redwoods, Douglas firs were waiting for us in Eugene, Oregon, two hundred miles away. They would be just as tall, though a bit more slender, and our challenge next time wouldn't be to take them lying flat on our backs. It would be for us to face them, climbing up.

Day 7: Eugene, Oregon, Climbing Trees

I become one, as the trees become many.
~ Hannah Witt, 2009

Before I start these next two chapters, I need to share something very personal, very revealing. For a longtime, I was afraid to commit this part of our story down on paper. I knew what a challenge it would be to write with words strong, vivid and detailed enough to describe what Cote and I experienced in Eugene, Oregon. This chapter you're about to read will bring my daughter and me face to face with the pinnacle of her rite of passage—the trees we have come to climb. In the next chapter you will read about us sleeping in them. It was one thing for us to ascend and explore these trees firsthand. It will be quite another to bring you up into the canopies with us.

Back in 2009, the day after our climb, I wrote eight pages of notes in my journal...eight pages. When I sit and reread those words today, I am taken back to that special place high overhead, sitting at the top of our Douglas fir. But my notes are a raw, jumbled mess—written in a form of shorthand that only I can understand. Thus, my challenge now is to bring these words to life, to breathe them into color along with all the sounds and smells the forest had to offer. If I am successful, you'll find yourself sitting on the branch of a tree far overhead, taking in a view few have ever seen. An ocean of green will spread out before you and you will be swept away by the beauty of it all. My hope is to get this right—for it is an honor to be the one to take you there.

The morning broke early in Eugene, Oregon. Inside our 1970-style Holiday Inn motel room, Cote and I bounded out of our beds, full of excitement and anticipation. This was it. The day of all days! The trees we've been waiting to climb were somewhere nearby and we were ready to find them.

We had booked our treetop adventure with the Pacific Tree Climbing Institute (PTCI), and Debbie, one of the owners, had given us some very helpful instructions for the morning of our climb. We were not to eat or drink too much. Staying hydrated was good, but she advised us against eating any foods that may upset our stomachs within twenty-four hours of climbing the trees. She also suggested we go easy on coffee and other beverages as well.

The detailed driving directions Debbie provided indicated we were only about twenty-five miles from the grove where we would climb. However, she also warned it would take us at least ninety minutes to get there from the town of Eugene. So, by eight o'clock in the morning, Cote and I had checked out of our motel room to begin navigating the backwoods of Oregon.

The roads we traveled twisted and turned and erased all sense of direction. Finding the exact spot to meet Jason, our guide, proved to be quite challenging, despite Debbie's impeccable directions. With the paved roads long gone and trees on every side, Cote and I began to second-guess our location. There were no signs, no markers, and no people.

Or rather, there was one person. A petite, dark-haired woman was leaning against a red Volvo when the dirt road we were traveling forked and split in two. As Cote and I edged by her car, we couldn't help but wonder what she was doing out here alone. We continued down the one-lane track, but soon the route became tangled with the Oregon outback and all but disappeared into the thick green foliage. We had no choice but to jockey our car around and head back to the split and to the woman who waited there. Maybe she could tell us where we were and point us in the right direction.

Her name was Jenny, and she told us she, too, was there to meet Jason. With three of us now waiting in the same remote location, we relaxed, feeling more confident we were in the right place. We passed the time by sharing who we were and why we'd come to climb trees. Jenny told us she was a single businesswoman from Los Angeles. She claimed that she wasn't the outdoorsy type, but told us every summer, she ventures out on vacation, alone in her Volvo, to explore new places. She spends her days hiking and her nights sleeping in her car. This, she explained, would be her first time ever climbing a tree.

Cote and Jenny hit it off from the moment we all met. I sat and watched as my eighteen-year-old daughter confidently engaged a stranger in a conversation that would not end until some twenty-four hours later. Jenny was a woman at least fifteen years older than Cote. She came from a totally different background and had already established a place for herself in the world. Yet, as these two shared their stories, I could tell Cote was growing as a young woman. Through their exchanges, my daughter was opening herself up to new ideas, thoughts, and possibilities. As a mother, I found the interaction remarkable to watch.

Twenty minutes later, Jason arrived. He pulled up in a very old, extremely used vehicle, and apologized repeatedly for being late. Car troubles, he explained—last minute and unexpected. He immediately began rushing around, pulling gear from his trunk. It was a good thing Jason was so quickly distracted after our introductions, or he would have seen the shocked expression openly broadcast upon my face.

I'm not sure what I expected our guide to look like, but Jason's appearance wasn't it. His shoulder-length blond hair was pulled back in a low ponytail and he was sporting a three-day beard. With his clothes looking as if he had slept in them for the past several nights, he had all the makings of being a long-lost hippie from the Sixties, although from what I could tell age-wise, he had to be in his early to mid-thirties. Given this first impression, I instantly began questioning his capabilities as a tree-climbing guide and I couldn't help but wonder what in the world I had gotten Cote and myself into.

Then Jason started talking about the trees, and I realized just how wrong I was going to be. With great enthusiasm, he shared his love for climbing. Jason spoke about being an arborist for the past fourteen years and how he had since perfected his trade. He reviewed our safety procedures and assured us that PTCI only provides the best in climbing gear. The man was totally prepared for the adventure at hand. His passion for nature was pure and contagious; his knowledge was comforting and reassuring. From the battered trunk of his car, he pulled out all our supplies—harnesses and rope, helmets and sleeping bags, water bottles and safety latches. Then he led us on a short hike through the forest to the famous Three Musketeers.

The trio of Douglas firs stood within an arm's length of each other. They were not particularly large in circumference, but they appeared strong and solid. Pointing to the one we would climb,

Jason informed us that it was 257 feet tall. We craned our necks upward but couldn't see the top. Ropes hanging down the sides of the trunk disappeared into the full, green canopy overhead, creating a secret hiding place waiting for us to discover.

Our lesson on tree-climbing was quick and very basic. Jason explained how the ropes could hold thousands of pounds, and our latches were safety-proof. We could climb up without worry of sliding back down. The mechanical teeth biting into the rope would prevent that from happening. At any given time, we could sit in our harnesses like a swing and relax. However, we had to work if we wanted to reach the top. By standing and pushing against the foot straps our bodies would move skyward. It would be a slow and methodical process, but eventually we'd get there.

"You won't really get the hang of it, though, until you just do it," Jason explained. "It will take trial and error and it might feel awkward at first. However, you'll be safe no matter what."

With those words spoken, there wasn't much left to say until we buckled in and started climbing.

We donned our helmets and harnesses, then clipped onto the ropes. Water bottles dangled from our belt loops as we pushed off one by one from the forest floor. Jenny took the lead, with Cote following close behind. I was grateful to let them both go first. We were clumsy, just like Jason said we'd be. We bobbled and wobbled in midair a mere foot or two off the ground. Soon, however, our feet and hands began to move in steady rhythm. We found our balance and slowly started making our way up the green giant, inch by inch.

At about fifty feet, I stopped to look back down. Jason had begun his own ascent. Clipped to his belt harness were all the things we'd need to spend the night: sleeping bags, pillows and three treeboats.

Jenny had told us when we first met that she had booked only the day climb, so she wouldn't be spending the night. She had a long drive back to Los Angeles and had to be at work early Monday morning. Thus, she'd have to say goodbye right after dinner tonight.

Watching as Jason expertly hoisted our gear higher and higher, I decided to slow my pace and wait for him to catch up. Cote and Jenny were already far above me, slipping out of sight inside the thickening branches. I knew they were racing each other to the top by the sound of their fading voices bantering back and forth. I couldn't help but feel a tiny bit jealous of their instant camaraderie. I had always imagined it would be Cote and me climbing side-by-side. Now, as I dangled in perfect solitude, I realized this was better for both of us. My daughter and I were at two completely different stages in life. It was right for us to climb these trees at our own personal pace, to find our unique and separate paths.

Cote was on the verge of crossing the threshold into a new and exciting world. She was full of youthful energy and ready to conquer. Her goal was to reach the top without stopping, to see all there was to see. She'd push through each thrilling moment and reach for the next higher branch to test her limits and her physical strength. She was anxious to arrive. Luckily, she had someone beside her who was looking to do the same.

My own reality was to go slow, to breathe, to take my time. The climb had to be savored so that all of my senses could share in the experience. I was looking for small details, tiny treasures, secret messages. Trees are a sacred symbol for me. From their hidden roots beneath the forest floor to their branches that stretch towards the sky, trees serve as a sign of God's presence and power in my life. Therefore, my spirit needed me to climb slowly.

As these thoughts dangled in the air with me, I realized both our pathways to the top held merit and worth. Cote's method of climbing was just as valid as mine, and vice versa. We each had our rightful approach; we both were honoring our inner voices. Eventually, we would sit side-by-side on top of the world, just like I had always imagined. However, we'd have our own story of arrival to tell.

My version would include Jason, who by now had caught up with me. For the next fifty- odd feet or so, I learned much about this man who climbed trees for a living. On any given day, he could see the world from an entirely different view, just by climbing up. He told me his greatest love was to bring children up into the canopies, especially school kids from the inner city. *Black tops to treetops,* he called it. His hope was to foster a love for nature in the next generation, as well as to help kids uncover some inner strengths and self-confidence. I asked a ton of questions, and Jason answered them all with patience and passion. I was the student; he was the teacher, sharing his knowledge and wisdom.

At 120 feet, we stopped. Jason told me this was where he would be hooking up our treeboats for the night. He needed to secure them in the light of day, so they would be ready for us when we returned to sleep in them that evening.

"Keep climbing. I'll meet you all at the top when I'm done," he said.

I continued on alone, up the side of this great giant. The higher I went, the more everything below me just melted away. The noises, the crazy roads, and the rush of life all disappeared. It was just this tree, with its simple beauty and quiet dignity, and me. I kept inching myself upward, stopping every so often to relax in my harness and take in the view. Somewhere around two hundred feet up the mighty trunk, a surprising thought hit me.

I am not afraid, not even a little bit.

Back when Cote and I were exploring the Rockies, I remembered how dizzy I felt whenever we walked to the edge of any given viewpoint and looked down. I recalled how nervous I'd become whenever I drove along the side of a mountain with no protective guardrail. Back then, the heights had given me chills, and I kept thinking, *How am I ever going to climb a tree? How am I going to strap on to a rope and climb 250 feet with my eyes open?*

Now here I was, doing just that, with absolutely no fear. Actually, what I felt was the complete opposite. I was filled with a calming sense of peace and security. With the tree as my anchor and the sky as my limit, I had a powerful urge to explore. I climbed with total abandon, searching the branches as I inched my way up, for nature's hidden treasures tucked within the crevices of bark and behind the dripping cascades of soft, green moss.

Although a typical description for something so beautiful would be to say, "It took my breath away," that's not how it was for me. Sitting in the upper-most branches of this super-tall tree, surrounded by an ocean of green, I felt as if I was taking my first true breath ever. The air I released from my lungs felt like it had been trapped inside me forever. Breathing up here was intoxicating, liberating. Every inhalation was fresh and pure and clean.

I rejoined Cote and Jenny at 230 feet, the highest point we would climb. Here we were invited to eat our lunch. The two girls were still chatting away, learning the finer details of each other's lives, as I settled in on a limb beside them. Seeing Cote perched so casually and comfortably on a branch at this elevation warmed my heart. I could tell she was enjoying this adventure as much as I was.

We opened our brown bags. To the delight of our hungry appetites, we discovered whole-wheat turkey and avocado sandwiches, all-natural potato chips, and crisp, red apples. Debbie, who in addition to being our coordinator was also Jason's wife, had packed our lunches with such care. Every bite was a delight to my taste buds.

It was strange, though, to be eating at the top of a tree. Tucked up against the solid trunk, with nothing but branches below and blue sky above, I felt like an eagle who had come home to his nest. Minutes into our lunch, Jason appeared. He asked how we were all doing and what we thought of the climb as he situated himself comfortably on his own branch and began to eat his lunch. There was a light breeze in the air, and the sun felt warm against our cheeks. With the branches thinned out at this height, it was amazing to see the vast, pillow-puffed treetops rolling for miles in every direction. I could have stayed here for hours enjoying the peaceful view, but all too soon Jason announced it was time for us to descend.

One by one, he switched the mechanisms on our harnesses from ascenders to descenders. Even though the changeover was quick, we were never "unlatched" completely during our transfers. Jason used secondary ropes to keep us safe and connected at all times.

The descender mechanism, he explained, was basically a pull-lever. Pull it down, and you'll go down; gravity will do all the work. Stop pulling, and you'll stop instantly, wherever and whenever you wanted to. If you pulled too hard, a safety catch would kick in and shut the gear down, so there was never any fear about falling too fast. We could descend as quickly as we wanted to, but I planned on taking it slow again. There was still so much to see, from the smallest of lichens growing on the rough-covered bark to the soft-green mosses dripping like molasses from every branch. The full mystery of this tree was at my fingertips, and I wanted to know its magic.

On our way down, we passed our sleeping quarters—the treeboats that would serve as our beds for the night. They looked comfortable enough now that they had been unfurled and fastened between the mighty tree trunk and three solid-looking limbs. After dinner, we would head back up the tree to sleep beneath the stars, tucked safely under our blankets made of branches and bark.

It was four o'clock in the afternoon when our toes finally touched the earth again. At first, it felt strange to be standing on solid ground. Our legs were numb and heavy, as the blood rushed back into our lower extremities. We unlatched our belts, stripped off our helmets, and stretched our languid limbs. We had well over an hour before Debbie was due to arrive with dinner, so Jason took us on a hike through the Oregon backwoods in search of a hidden stream he had found once before.

The forest enveloped us from all sides. Dense ferns brushed against our open palms, soft and lush. The soil beneath our feet was dark and smelled earthy. The towering trees closed in, powerful and protective. Jason's sense of direction soon led us to the rippling stream, with its cool water and glittering stones. We fanned out and explored on our own for a while, each of us lost in quiet thought. After our time of wandering, Jason gathered us like baby chicks and we followed him back to camp.

Debbie was waiting for us with a spread fit for a king: pasta with homemade spaghetti sauce, a fresh green salad with ingredients straight from her garden, and warm homemade bread. For dessert, she had baked a Marianne Berry pie, the fruit being native to their Oregon area, a cross between a raspberry and blueberry.

Every bite was an explosion of flavor upon my tongue. We all ate with gusto, filling our plates and going back for seconds. The best part of the evening, however, was finally meeting Debbie in person. I had spoken with her several times on the phone as I planned our climb, but wasn't expecting her to be our chef and hostess, too. Cote and I were thrilled to have the opportunity to thank her in person for all her help. She was a gentle soul with a constant smile, warm and inviting and as natural as the Oregon trees surrounding us. She and Jason made a perfect pair; they loved their work and enjoyed sharing the trees with those who came to climb them.

The four of us could have talked all night, while sitting in our comfortable lawn chairs, as dusk slowly settled in around us. But we were also anxious to head back up into the canopies for our night of sleeping in the trees. That's when Jenny dropped her bomb.

"I can't leave now. I just can't. I have to stay and sleep up there with you guys."

What? Is she serious? How could she stay? Jenny was facing a thirteen-hour drive home, and she had to report to work first thing Monday morning. Staying here tonight and lingering over a Sunday breakfast would leave her with a terribly long day of driving tomorrow. Besides, there were only three treeboats hanging 120 feet above our heads. Night was falling quickly, and hoisting another bed up at this hour would be no easy undertaking. I couldn't believe what I was hearing, but Jenny was adamant about her decision.

"How can I come this far and not stay? I know I have a long drive home, but I'll worry about that tomorrow," she told us. "If I don't spend the night tonight, I may never do this again."

With that final declaration, we all began to scurry. Cote, Jenny, and I helped Debbie pack up the dishes, while Jason grabbed another treeboat from his trunk. He was amazing. Despite Jenny's unexpected bombshell and all the extra work now ahead of him, he never once complained. Instead, he remained calm, cool and directed. True to character, Jason's only goal was to help others come to a deep appreciation for nature and the beauty of these trees. He would do whatever it took to get Jenny settled in for the sleepover of her life.

After the dishes were done and the supplies were packed, we quickly readied ourselves for the night and our final climb. The sun was sitting low in the sky as we began our ascent. For the next twelve hours, Cote and I would be immersed in a world neither of us ever dreamed of entering. It would be a night full of mysterious sights and sounds and sensations. We would fall asleep cradled in the arms of tree branches and blanketed by soft, green mosses. The forest would sing us its lullabies. Feeling like a child heading up to bed, I couldn't wait to be tucked in.

Day 8: Eugene, Oregon, Sleeping in Trees

A tree house, a free house, a secret you and me house,
A high up in the leafy branches, cozy as can be house.
A street house, a neat house, be sure and wipe your feet
house,
Is not my kind of house at all—let's go live in a tree house.
~Shel Silverstein, *Where the Sidewalk Ends*

The night closed in around us as we climbed our way back up the trees. Jason carried one more treeboat while the rest of us were free of any extra baggage. We were dressed in warm, loose clothing, and we had taken care of all our bedtime "routines" down below, from brushing our teeth to emptying our bladders. We had twelve long hours ahead of us, suspended 120 feet in the air. Heaven forbid any of us should have the urge to *go* at any point during the night. If that happened, we had three options: 1.) Discreetly use a Freshette (small plastic device) while crouched in our treeboat, 2.) Wake Jason and the two of us would climb down to conduct the business on the forest floor, or 3.) Hold it.

Needless to say, none of these choices sounded very appealing or pleasant.

Luckily, the higher we climbed, the more our personal hygiene anxieties faded away. The trees closed in and closed off all our worries and cares. We were surrounded, 360 degrees, by the towering green giants. Distractions dissolved one by one and were replaced by simple peace and tranquility. With the sun finally beneath the horizon, only a few golden streaks of amber were left in the sky, softly brushing our skin and blurring the sharp edges of bark and needle.

The night turned still, and the air turned cooler. Yet what surprised me the most was that the encroaching darkness lacked anything eerie or frightening. No scary sounds punctured the forest's black curtain, nor did frightening shadows appear against the trunk of our tree. Feeling safe and secure, Cote and Jenny decided to climb all the way back up to the top, while Jason stopped at our sleeping station to hook-up the fourth treeboat. I decided to hang back to see if I could be of any help. I managed to hold a few loose ropes and gadgets for Jason while he tightened straps and leveled the hammock into place.

When the treeboat was finished, Jason started up the trunk once more to fetch Cote and Jenny. They were sitting in the dark canopy overhead waiting for him to come switch their gears to descenders so they could climb back down. At first, the girls' voices had echoed loud and clear off the quiet trees as they moved upward into the thick, heavy boughs. Now all that remained were a few faint whispers drifting down to me through the night air.

I decided to get my treeboat ready for sleeping while my three companions were gone. I spread out my bedroll and plumped up my pillow upon my canvas hammock. It was a slow moving process, having to crouch on one end of the treeboat while I worked the bedding into place on the other. The hammock hardly moved at all, though. Jason had expertly attached it tightly and securely to the trunk of the tree.

Getting into my sleeping bag turned out to be more difficult than I thought it would be. The safety harness strapped around my waist bunched and gathered as I tried to slide into my flannel cocoon. The rope attached to my belt needed to dangle over the side of the hammock, where I had three feet of slack before the lead rope would catch and prevent any fall. With all this safety gear, zipping up my sleeping bag was not an option. I simply pulled my top cover over me as best I could, and then settled in.

That was when everything turned quiet and still. My breathing slowed and in the silence of my surroundings, my mind began to replay the day. Suddenly, I wanted my journal and pen; I felt an overwhelming urge to physically record the day's events. I used my clip light to illuminate the duffle bag Jason had carried up earlier. Both my writing utensils were buried at the bottom of it. The bag, however, was hanging from another branch, a good two feet away. At that distance, I was too afraid to lean and grab for it, and even more afraid I'd drop my journal should I actually get my hands on it. If that happened, my notebook would lay vulnerable 120 feet below me on the forest floor for the rest of the night. I couldn't bear the thought of a nocturnal animal chewing through my pages, tearing my words away.

So I fought to commit the stories of today to memory, instead. That was like trying to lasso wild horses, however, as there was so much galloping through my mind. I replayed our day over and over again, exhausting every last detail. I memorized our conversations and relived how it felt to climb so high.

Once again, I breathed in the crisp, clean air, the heady smell of pine. I mentally noted how beautiful the mid-afternoon views were, and how the sea of trees flowed forever when I sat upon the topmost branch and scanned the horizon. I recalled how hidden I felt from the world below me, and how freeing it was to be anchored to a tree. I remembered the rough bark beneath my fingertips and the soft moss dripping through outstretched branches. I recalled how safe I felt climbing, and I noticed now how comfortable the treeboat was cradling my tired but happy body. I was wrapped like a baby in the caring embrace of this mothering tree.

As these memories drifted through my mind, my body began to relax even more. Every muscle, every fiber let go and melted into the canvas seams of my bedding. The physical demands of the day and the cooling air of the night brought sleep. By the time my companions returned, I was already floating in dreamland. The rustling sounds they made were miles away, but their soft, tired voices soothed me like the ending of a bedtime story.

The last thing I heard was the hooting of an owl, several trees over. Something in his tone reminded me how honored I should feel to share such a sacred and holy place with him.

How long I'd been asleep, I couldn't tell, but when I awoke I was shocked to find a bright light shining down on me. *Is it morning already? Have I really slept the whole night away?* The branches above me were cast in a dazzling white glow. Twigs and needles were haloed in angelic light. I blinked my eyes and into focus came a brilliant silver sphere. The moon! Piercing the night, its glow lit up the canopy around me, giving me a rare and extraordinary view of the midnight forest.

Grateful that it wasn't yet morning and that I still had time in these majestic trees, I settled back into my treeboat and gave thanks for my unexpected awakening. My friendly area hoot owl called out again, perhaps just to let me know he, too, was awake and enjoying the show. What a relief to realize I still had plenty of night left ahead of me. I wasn't ready for my time in the trees to end.

I snuggled deeper into my sleeping bag and tucked the fabric under my chin. The air was cooler than when I'd first fallen asleep, but still not cold. I felt refreshed from my couple hours of sleep and comfortable in my surroundings. The canopy was quiet all around me. Not one mosquito buzzed within earshot. Jason had told us earlier these pesky vampires don't normally venture higher than thirty feet above the forest floor, but at the moment no other flying insect seemed to be either. The only creature we needed to brace ourselves for, Jason warned, was a tree mouse. So far, so good, though. None of those seemed to be stirring as well.

I stayed awake for quite some time, mesmerized by the gentleness of the forest. It was bizarre to feel so at home, so at ease, in such a strange and isolated place. I wished we could stay longer—another night or even a week. I felt sense a sense of tranquility like never before up here.

Eventually, the urge to sleep returned, with a soft pecking at the back of my eyelids. Though I hated to give in, I couldn't continue the fight. So I closed my eyes once more.

Around five o'clock in the morning my internal alarm clock clicked on, reawakening me. I wasn't in a hurry to start moving around too much, however. We weren't supposed to descend the trees until Debbie arrived with our breakfast, and that wouldn't be until eight o'clock. Three hours would be a long time to wait, should my bladder decide to kick in, so in hopes of keeping that need at bay, I closed my eyes again and prayed this time for sleep to come find me.

Just after six o'clock, I knew I was awake for good. The sun was breaking through the trees to the east, warming the air, and stirring the forest to life. Birds were fluttering in twos and threes overhead, briefly landing on branches and pushing off again in search of breakfast. I watched them in silent reverie. From my vantage point, I was a secret spectator to their morning activities, an undetected observer within their secluded backyard.

The other three treeboats, all hanging just higher than mine, were quiet and calm. Since I couldn't see inside them, I couldn't tell if my companions were also lying awake enjoying the magic of morning breaking open like I was. Spying my camera dangling from a clasp at the foot of my hammock, I leaned forward and unhooked it. With such a rare and beautiful view of the coming sunrise, I couldn't think of a better way to pass the time than to capture it in pictures.

Just after seven o'clock the other treeboats began to sway softly, one by one. Cote was the first to lift her sleepyhead, and I was ready to greet her with an enthusiastic, "Good morning, Sunshine," followed by a digital snap of her profile. Not ready to receive such a lively welcome, she immediately flopped back into her boat and let out a muddled groan. To my right, Jenny sat up and began to stretch and yawn. Higher up above us all, I could hear Jason beginning to rustle as well.

Everyone's movements were slow and unhurried. There was no reason for us to rush; we had plenty of time to enjoy this new day dawning. It wasn't until the sound of an approaching car broke through the soft sounds of nature that we began to move with more intention. No one would be this far back into the woods, at this hour of the day except for Debbie. Surely it was she, arriving with our breakfast.

What happened next was hard to believe.

Jason climbed out of his boat and made his way to a dangling rope that seemed to have appeared overnight. Calling out to Debbie below, the two of them put into motion a pulley system, with Jason tugging up whatever it was that Debbie had packed in the basket below. Higher and higher the basket rose, as we peered over the edges of our treeboats in great anticipation. Within minutes, a care package arrived to our lofty perch. It contained a thermos and three terry-soft white washcloths.

Jason opened the canister and poured its contents onto each of the three towels. As he handed a cloth to each of us, the smell of peppermint wafted through the air. The warm, wet, scented towel in my hand was heavenly. I washed the sleep from my face and pressed the cloth to my nose to breathe in deeper its pure, fresh scent. What an unexpected luxury in such a primitive, remote setting.

Jason lowered the basket back to Debbie and she refilled it. Two more thermoses came up, this time with coffee and juice for all of us. I could not believe the pampering we were receiving so high up above the world. I love coffee; I can't imagine starting my day without it. Yet this felt like a dream—sitting in a treeboat, sipping hot coffee, in the cool, crisp hours of morning, while casually conversing with my fellow climbers about our night. The entire scene was completely bizarre and incredibly wonderful.

The rest of our morning continued in much the same fashion— slow, and with many unexpected and pleasant surprises. We packed up our night gear and descended down to the forest floor one final time. In a way, I couldn't help but feel like an astronaut returning to earth after a trip around the moon. I found my reentry heavy and burdensome. It was hard to let go of that weightless place I had discovered at 120 feet in the air.

Debbie was there to soften my landing, though. She had packed a light organic breakfast, which we ate with full attention, once again savoring every bite. By eleven o'clock, it was time to begin our goodbyes. Jenny had a long day of driving south ahead of her, and Cote and I needed to begin our journey east.

After eighteen months of planning and waiting, my daughter and I had done what we'd said we'd do: we climbed and slept in the tree of our dreams. Now it was time to turn our car towards home. I had no doubt that plenty of adventure was still ahead of us, though. We had seven more days of traveling strange and new roads, leading to detours and discoveries. But the pinnacle of Cote's rite of passage would now be behind us. With heartfelt thanks and a circle of hugs, we said our goodbyes to Jason, Debbie, and Jenny.

It took an hour and a half to backtrack out of the Oregon woods and slip onto Route 58 East. Once we hit the two-lane highway, we picked up speed. There was no traffic on this Sunday afternoon to slow us down. Moving fast didn't feel right, though—not after such an emotion-packed twenty-four hours.

It wasn't long before the small-town of Willamette Pass came into view, along with a little log cabin-style motel sitting alone and quiet by the edge of the road. The place immediately caught our attention, snapping our necks around as we sped by. It was quaint. It was cozy. What's more, there wasn't a single car in the gravel parking lot. Although it was only 3:30 in the afternoon and we had hours of daylight left to drive, this place looked too perfect. It was just what Cote and I needed to reflect and regroup. I swung my head in her direction and exhaled my burning question, "What do you think?"

"Let's do it," she replied.

Without hesitation, I turned the car around. Ten minutes later, Cote and I checked in as the only guests of the Willamette Pass

Inn. We grabbed our backpacks and journals from the car. We took a couple of hot showers and put on our flannel pajamas. Then we settled in for a lazy, laid-back Sunday afternoon.

I spent my time writing down all those thoughts I had before falling asleep in the trees. Cote spent some time with her friends on Facebook, catching up on the latest happenings back home and filling them in on her most recent adventure out west. When hunger pains kicked in, we walked to the almost empty tavern next door and picked up a basket of chicken to take back to our room. Our evening closed out quietly. Cote and I had two warm beds to curl up in and four solid walls to protect us. The unknowns of the night were safely locked outside our door. As I fell asleep secure inside the comforts of our small, well-equipped room, I couldn't help but wonder what was happening in those tall, wild trees of yesterday.

*For pictures of our tree-climbing adventure, as well as other photos from our two-week rite of passage, please go to: *www. rootedtogether-jolenewitt.blogspot.com*

Day 9: Willamette Pass, Oregon to St. Anthony, Idaho, 686 miles

You gain strength, courage, and confidence by every experience
in which you really stop to look fear in the face.
You must do the thing which you think you cannot do.
~Eleanor Roosevelt

When Cote and I opened the door to our motel room at 7:15 this morning, we stepped into a world of shock—a cold snap, registering thirty-eight bone-chilling degrees! *What the heck? Isn't this still August?* The artic blast had us sprinting for the car. We threw our bags into the back, and then jumped into the front, shivering as our bodies slid across the cold leather seats. Our teeth chattered like wind-up toys and our hands shook as we cupped them to our mouths, trying to warm them with our breaths. I started the engine, cranked the heat, and turned the car east out of the motel's driveway. I couldn't believe how cold it was, and I couldn't be more thankful this drop in temperature had held off one more day. Otherwise, Cote and I would have been two frozen icicles stuck to the branch of a 257-foot Douglas fir tree this morning.

We spent the day driving, logging almost seven hundred miles by the time we pulled over for the night. We were both well rested after yesterday's laid-back afternoon and last night's full eight hours of sleep. More importantly, my mind was now fully at rest, too. I had been attacked by a pretty profound moment of panic last night around seven o'clock. It snuck up on me while I was journaling and grabbed me by total surprise.

I was writing about our tree climbing experience with our fold-out map spread open on the coffee table in front of me. Glancing at the atlas of the United States on full display, the reality of our cross-country trip hit me for the very first time. I realized just how far away from home Cote and I had traveled. *Three thousand miles.* Three thousand long and dangerous miles lay between the Willamette Pass Inn and the safety of our front door back home. We were two women traveling alone in a car. So many things could have gone wrong already—and so many other things still might.

The weight of this reality came crashing down on me last night. Fear broke in and stole all my confidence. Before I knew what was happening, my mind was rifling through a long list of what-ifs: *What if one of us gets sick? Or hurt? What if our car breaks down? Or we blow a tire? What if something terrible happens while we're crossing a backcountry road, deep inside a cellular dead zone?*

Under the burden of all these terrifying thoughts, my lungs squeezed shut, expelling all the air from my chest. I doubled over in a wave of nausea. I tried my best to camouflage what was happening to me by making my movements appear as normal as I could in case Cote glanced my way. I slowly dropped my gaze and turned my head to the window, shielding my contorted face. I reached forward to refold the map as my body folded over in its state of shock. I couldn't let Cote see me like this. I didn't want to scare her too.

Sitting sideways in my chair, with my back to my daughter, I struggled to take several deep and calming breaths. I forced my mind to concentrate on only the good things—why we were here in the first place and all the wonderful memories we'd made so far. I closed my eyes and relived the miles Cote and I had covered together. I thought about all the days behind us and the days yet to come.

Then I tipped my head and began to pray. Inside our little room at the unassuming Willamette Pass Inn, I asked God for strength and courage. I begged for trust and tenacity. We were halfway through Cote's rite of passage—I knew in my heart, we were right where we belonged. I prayed that fear would not take any of this away from me—not now, not ever. I asked for strength to fight its destructive pull and resist the urge to rush us home, the one place I have always felt safe. I petitioned God to help me feel that same sense of security right here, three thousand long miles away.

The prayers started to work. My mind began to ease and release its panic. As it did, a deeper truth seeped and settled into the space that was created. I realized it was okay for me to be scared. Without fear, I wouldn't grow as a person of faith. Without fear, I wouldn't recognize the courage I do have. This trip had already required great faith and courage from both Cote and me. We had come all this way and we had done amazing things. Fear had been a factor for us at times, but never a limiter. By putting the emotion to good use, Cote and I had discovered places of great beauty, grace, and possibility. It was okay for me to feel fear; I just couldn't let it lead the way.

Last night, before I fell asleep in our lonely motel room far from home, I tucked fear into the most remote corner of my mind. This morning, I gave it a place in the backseat with the rest of our luggage, knowing at times I would need small servings of it, when particular situations warranted mindfulness and caution. What I would not do, however, was give fear any room in the driver's seat with me.

Conversation between us was light and breezy as Cote and I traveled the open road today. We simply relaxed into the ride with each passing mile, heading towards Yellowstone, our next major destination. The park was still too faraway to reach in a single day, but we pushed the pedal and ourselves to get as close as we could. We fell short by eighty miles when we decided to pull over for the night in St. Anthony, Idaho, the last sizable town on our map before reaching Yellowstone's western gate. Cote and I knew we could easily finish the drive in the morning and then have the rest of the day to play inside the national park.

Despite the day's relaxed atmosphere, we did have one "lightbulb" moment. While driving along a quiet stretch of Highway 20, I realized Cote and I had not hugged each other for the past several days. This hit me as very strange, since it was such a daily occurrence in our routine lives back home. A typical day for us meant spending eight to ten hours apart, due to work and school. But before the day was over, we'd come together, hug, and say, "I missed you," or "Goodnight." Crisscrossing the country together on this trip, however, had now joined us at the hip, twenty-four hours a day. Thus, this tender mother-daughter ritual had subconsciously been left abandoned along the roadside of Cote's rite of passage.

"You know what, Cote? I haven't hugged you for days."

"You know what? You're right. You haven't."

"Isn't that weird? I think because we've been together so much, I haven't really thought about it until now. I mean, we talk, we hike, we climb, we drive. And then at the end of the day, we say goodnight. We fall asleep without having to leave the room. I just realized how much I miss hugging you. So when we pull over tonight, I'm going to give you the biggest hug ever."

"Okay. And then when you're done, I'm going to give you one."

We kept our promises and shared those hugs inside our motel room in St. Anthony, Idaho. I wish I could say this is how our day ended, with a mother and daughter sharing such a simple, loving gesture, but I can't. There was another emotion-filled night coming my way. This time it wasn't fear that grabbed me. It was irritation.

Cote and I cleaned up and settled into our evening. Once again, I opened my notebook to journal, and she opened her laptop to Facebook. Tonight, however, the techno-world my daughter stepped into began to aggravate me on a level I hadn't expected or experienced before. As Cote clicked and typed, I felt like I was losing her. It was as if she was being led down some private, secretive path that didn't include me or respect her rite of passage. What made it worse—she seemed to go willingly.

As the night wore on, a coma-like trance came over her. Cote was so engrossed in her multiple online conversations, that she was completely oblivious to the silent but furious one I was having with her inside my head. Despite my rising anger, I refused to give a voice to my objections. Stubbornly I felt that after eighteen years of living together, my daughter should be fully capable of reading all my thoughts and deciphering my body language clues. *Obviously, I'm speaking loud and clear. Why, then, can't she hear me?*

I rolled over and closed myself off. Eventually, I fell into a restless, fitful sleep. Cote's online socializing and my refusal to address it poked a pin-sized hole into what I had thought to be our impenetrable mother-daughter relationship. Little did I know, the puncture wound wouldn't lead to a slow and steady leak. It would be the opening to our biggest blowout ever.

Day 10: St. Anthony, Idaho to Yellowstone National Park, 80 miles

To text or not to text...this seems to be our biggest issue, our most challenging roadblock.
~Excerpt from Jolene's journal, Tuesday night, August 11, 2009.

Irritated. Frustrated. Annoyed. That's how I woke up on the morning of Day 10—with these three emotions still pulsing through my veins. I decided to remain quiet, however, about Cote's computer usage and my resulting dark midnight mood. I was hoping this new day would signal a new start. Besides, maybe it was just me being too sensitive in all of this. After all, the techno-communication gap that stretched like a huge, black hole between us, was my doing—not Cote's. *Maybe I just need to lighten up,* I thought.

Bright sunshine, blue skies, and a clear highway greeted us as we pulled the car out of the motel parking lot and headed towards Yellowstone. The first forty-five minutes were smooth sailing. We drove along in peaceful companionship, enjoying nature's scenery and the quiet morning unfolding. Then at nine o'clock, Cote's cell phone began buzzing.

With speed and precision, her fingers started flying across the tiny keypad in her hand. Oblivious to my frustration from the night before, Cote eagerly picked up a conversation with some invisible person somewhere in the world—I was assuming a friend back home. Hearing the *click, click, clicking* sound again instantly refueled my emotions. I fought against my rising temper, somehow managing to successfully count to ten. Then, hoping to pull my daughter back into the seat beside me, I asked a light and leading question, "Something up?"

"No, not really. Just Liz."

Silence. Minutes passed. Cote offered nothing more. She simply continued to type and pause as she conversed with her best friend on the other end of her mini-keyboard. I counted to fifty, and then I tried to light the flame of conversation between us again, "Everything all right?"

"Huh? Oh...yeah...fine."

Her fingers flew over the keyboard once more and my temper ignited red-hot. No amount of counting could extinguish the flames burning inside my brain now.

What happened next was fast and out of control. Words exploded, hot and ugly. What was said, exactly? I don't recall. All I do remember is our emotions going from zero to sixty in about 2.2 seconds flat.

I snapped. Cote snapped. She yelled. I shouted.

Unleashing my hidden cell-phone fury, I threw out everything I had kept bottled up for days and Cote fired back with a force just as strong and stubborn. We fought for our ground. We gave as good as we got, trying to win inch after inch of battlefield in our war of words.

Ten miles from the gates of Yellowstone, Cote abruptly ended the argument by launching a cold and definitive, "Whatever!" across the front seat. It hit me square in the chest and stunned my heart.

Refusing to be outdone, I quickly camouflaged my shock and flung my own icy "Whatever!" back at her.

Immediately the air between us drew tight. Our lungs locked up. Neither of us could breathe.

As if a coffin lid had slammed shut upon our car, those two words nailed us in. We were sealed inside with no way of escape. All sympathy, empathy, and understanding disappeared, as Cote and I turned cold and unforgiving. We became two people I had never met before.

Right then the western gates of Yellowstone came into view. With lips shut tight, no reaction erupted from either one of us. I stopped at the ranger booth to pay for our day's pass and had to wonder what the park attendant thought. As I lowered my window, the only emotion that poured from inside our vehicle was a cold wave of indifference. There was no excitement in my voice, no giddiness from my traveling companion. I simply dumped the money in his hand.

When the ranger wished us a good day, I scarcely nodded and Cote's nose remained pressed against the passenger side window. Physically we had arrived; emotionally we were miles away.

I pulled the car through the entryway and my eyes flicked across a "no vacancy" sign regarding the park's lodging and campsites for the night. *So what?* I thought. That little tidbit of information didn't pertain to us. Yesterday Cote and I had decided we would only spend the day in Yellowstone. Our plan was to see three main attractions—Old Faithful, Artist Point, and Mount Washburn—and we'd stay only as long as it took to see them. Then we'd leave the park by the north gate and find a place to sleep. Knowing what our plan was, I drove through the entranceway, not having to speak to my daughter or get her opinion on where to go first. I just opened our park map and found the road that would lead us to Old Faithful.

A mile or two into Yellowstone, the cold and indifferent atmosphere inside our car was still locked in place. It took some dogged determination on both our parts, but it was obvious neither wanted to be the first to shed her shield of stubbornness. Even the dazzling beauty of Yellowstone couldn't warm our hearts and melt the frozen glacier that had slid into the front seat between us. Cote and I drove on, looking at everything, but not seeing a thing.

Then around the next bend, traffic came to a complete stop.

I knew what the long line of stalled cars meant. There was a sighting up ahead, a wild animal of some kind—a bird, a bison, an elk, or maybe a moose. Something had caught everyone's attention, slowing traffic to a snail's crawl.

I also knew it could be miles before we'd reach the excitement. People at the front of the line would take their time. They'd pull over to the side of the road and snap their fill of pictures. I knew what was happening, but Cote didn't. I could tell by her shifting body language that she was growing irritated. She didn't understand what the hold-up was all about. I could have easily clued her in but in my juvenile, foolish state of mind, I felt as if I now held the upper hand. We continued to inch forward in silence.

Finally we reached the prize: a bald eagle perched high in a leafless tree. The bird was majestic in his contrast of black and white against a cloudless blue sky. With his breast puffed out and his eagle eyes sharp, he appeared ready for anything. He sat scanning the beauty all around him, taking it all in. Though it was a crazy idea, I couldn't help but think this bird had been planted to teach Cote and me a lesson. We shouldn't be letting anything, especially a silly disagreement, spoil our view of the beauty all around us. We were fortunate to be here. None of what we were seeing should ever be taken for granted.

I wanted to voice these thoughts, but I wasn't ready to give in. I continued to hold my tongue even through a second sighting—this time a couple young elk grazing along the roadside. We crawled our way past the impressive animals, stuck in our self-imposed quagmire of silence. It was obvious Cote and I were hating every minute of this. We even refused to take pictures, knowing it would require setting our guard down in order to pick up the camera.

At the next intersection we turned right, losing a good chunk of traffic. We continued our trek towards Old Faithful, but I was slowly dying inside. I couldn't believe Cote and I had stuck to our guns for this long. It was awful, terrible, agonizing. Every mile that passed, was one more mile lost forever between us.

How much longer will this last? What will it take to pull us back together again?

That's when it hit me. I was the one in the driver's seat. I was the one in control of how far we took this. With a simple turn of the steering wheel and a push of the brake, I could put a stop to this mid-morning madness. I could lay the first stone to bridge this mother-daughter impasse.

Just ahead there was a sign for an upcoming mini geyser, not the grand Old Faithful, but a much smaller preview to the main attraction. I pulled into the parking lot and circled all the way around, finding an open space to park at the far end. People were filing out of their cars, making their way down a wooden boardwalk to the hot spring over a nearby ridge, and just out of view. I shoved the car in park, but left the engine running, keeping the two of us locked inside.

Shifting in my seat I turned to face my daughter. Calmly I

began to speak, from my heart and from my point of view. I shared with Cote the highest hopes I had dreamed for us, and my deep disappointment over what had displaced us. Thankfully, she was ready to receive my words and share her own point of view.

We took turns voicing our feelings, speaking our peace. As we did, the tightness inside our car exhaled and we felt as wide open and clean as Yellowstone itself. Cote and I built the bridge and closed the gap between us. To our relief, we found healing and forgiveness on the other side. We acknowledged each other's rights and we accepted our own wrongs. We recognized our "human-ness" by admitting we were bound to make mistakes. Two powerful words spoken by us both finally healed the angry "whatever's" we had thrown at each other earlier—"I'm sorry."

Cote and I hugged and smiled. Then as the healing continued to settle into our souls, I put the car into gear and began to back it up.

"What are you doing? Aren't we going to get out and go see Old Faithful?"

"Yeah, but this isn't it. This is just a little hot spring. A preview to Old Faithful, which is farther down the road."

"Oh. I thought we were here. I thought that was it." She pointed to a small puff of smoke rising above the dry, white-colored mound of sand.

"No, Cote. That ain't it. In fact, you ain't seen nothing yet..."

Yellowstone: Old Faithful, 11:00 a.m.

*When you pray, be open to the answer. Never assume that
it will come in the color you ordered. The hardest thing is
recognizing the answer when it's not only NOT the color you
asked for, but not even the right size.*
~ Excerpt from Mary Weeber's Rite of Passage letter

We had a "Claritin-clear" kind of moment. Just like the commercial on television that pulls back the dull film from the corner of the screen, Yellowstone became vibrant, sharp and full of color. With the toxic air removed and the layer of grime over our eyes scrubbed clean, Cote and I could breathe again. We could see again.

From then on, the massive park became a wide-open adventureland full of wildlife and beauty. Cote and I drank it in. We pushed ourselves to experience as much as possible without missing the magic of any given moment. We were fully present to each other and to the gifts of nature all around us. The next twenty-seven hours proved to be incredible—yes, twenty-seven.

Cote and I ended up spending the night inside Yellowstone. Our original plan of sight-seeing for only a day flew out our back window around 4:30 in the afternoon. For this morning, however, we were right on schedule and headed for Old Faithful.

The giant geyser appeared to be a popular first choice for many. In fact, it seemed everyone inside Yellowstone had come to this exact same spot at the exact same time. The colossal parking lot was packed with row after row of vehicles—cars, trucks, motorcycles, campers, and tour buses. Huge buildings formed the perimeter of the attraction, including an enormous hotel, several gift shops, concession stands, and an interactive visitor center. Old Faithful was leaving nothing to chance.

The sun was hot and the crowd was thick when Cote and I exited our car and moved into the mix of people. After checking the information sign for the geyser's next scheduled outburst, we wandered around the complex, following the wave of bodies. The area was certainly touristy, with its buildings and boardwalks, benches and bystanders. Once again, Cote and I felt out of place with all the materialism, but we did manage to get some of our gift shopping done. We purchased a few small tokens for loved ones back home. Then we wandered back outside into the folds of people and waited for the spring to build up steam.

When Old Faithful finally did its thing—when a flying spray of hot steam erupted from beneath the dry, crusty ground and shot into the air—Cote and I simply stood and watched. There were no spontaneous *oohs* or *ahhs* from either of us. To be honest, the old geyser left us feeling a little let down. Cote snapped a few obligatory pictures, but once the show was over, we glanced at each other with looks that said, "Huh. So, that was it?"

Old Faithful wasn't as impressive as I had remembered it to be, but in all fairness, I was a child the last time I saw it. At twelve years of age, this geyser seemed to loom large over me. Now as an adult, Old Faithful still possessed a certain unique and rare charm, but its grandeur had lost some of its size. Maybe it was the man-made structures surrounding this rightful point of interest. The towering grand hotel, for instance, dwarfed the phenomenon taking place right in front it. After the geyser's spouting ended, Cote and I looped arms and headed back to the car. We were anxious to move on, excited to see more of Yellowstone. There was, however, one short yet reflective conversation that took place just as we were exiting the parking lot.

"Okay, so we both agree that Old Faithful wasn't that great. But you know what, Cote? We could use Old Faithful to remind of us of something much bigger, much more powerful, and forever faithful in our lives."

"I already know where you're going with this, Mom."

"Oh yeah? And where's that?"

"You're talking about God."

"Oooh, okay. You're so smart. But you know what? He's the original Old Faithful, isn't He? Maybe that's what we're supposed to take away with us today."

Even though Old Faithful didn't rock our Richter scale, nothing could dampen our mood. Cote and I were ready for adventure, so we took off farther and deeper into Yellowstone. Following the map, we took the turnoff that would lead us to Artist Point. We really didn't know what this name signified, but we were both anxious and excited to find out.

Along the way, Cote and I made one or two unexpected stops to take some pictures and do a little exploring. One place, in particular—Yellowstone Lake—turned out to be a hidden treasure, a quiet relief from the bustling crowds and hustling traffic.

Cote and I discovered the oasis when the road we were traveling curved and began following the lake's natural edge. The alluring blue water, the pebble-strewn shoreline, and the sun glittering on the surface like a thousand diamond chips were all just too much to resist. As soon as we came upon a deserted stretch of roadway, I pulled the car over. The embankment leading down to the lake was steep, so Cote and I slid on our backsides all the way to the bottom. The water, the sky, and the soft gentle breezes were just the right mixture of ingredients to feed our adventurous souls.

Cote found a large piece of driftwood, where she could practice a makeshift balance beam routine, tiptoeing her way out from the edge of the lake. Meanwhile, I tossed rocks into the water at her feet, trying to splash and throw her off-kilter. She was amazing to watch. Agile, giddy and childlike, her eyes danced, reflecting the crystal-clear water and the endless possibility of youth.

Watching my daughter teeter back and forth upon that log, I couldn't help but think about how she and I would teeter across the next twelve months. The year ahead would be a tightrope of learning, balancing the old with the new. Cote and I would have to reshape and redefine our mother-daughter relationship as she entered the world of college, the realm of new challenges and change. It would be foolish of me to think our every step would be sure-footed and solid. Sooner or later, difficulties would come, and one or both of us might slip and fall.

Standing along this lakeshore today, I remembered we had a powerful tool ready and willing to help us. Faith. With our faith in God and in each other, we could make it across any rocky terrain or unsteady bridge that came our way. Cote and I would need to keep our safety ropes secure and our lines of communication open. But if we did, I was positive we'd find ourselves on the other side of next year, hand in hand and heart-to-heart, with our feet firmly planted in the soil of tomorrow.

I was jolted out of my distant thoughts when other sightseers began to arrive at our secluded hideaway. I think our playfulness along the shoreline caught their attention from the road, and the lure of the lake was just as strong and inviting to them as it had been for us. In any case, their arrival meant it was time for us to go. Cote and I raced back up the hill, feeling refreshed from our exploring and eager to find the next adventure that Yellowstone had in-store.

Yellowstone: Artist Point, 2:00 p.m.

The finest workers in stone are not copper or steel tools, but the gentle touches of air and water working at their leisure with a liberal allowance of time.
~Henry David Thoreau

It is becoming next to impossible for me to put Yellowstone into words. Cote and I had only been inside the park for four hours, and already I was running out of ways to describe its wonders. Everything so far had been an explosion to the mind, a blast to all five senses: rich landscapes, peaceful prairies, bold rock formations, and clear forest streams. This place contains nature at its absolute finest. By the time Cote and I finished our twenty-seven hours of exploring, we had touched only a tiny portion of Yellowstone's 2.2 million-plus-acre-wonderland. What we took in and what we took away, however, will be inked forever inside the sketchbook of my soul.

Cote and I took the turn-off for Artist Point at two o'clock this afternoon. The parking lot was almost full and the sun was blazing hot, but thankfully a comfortable breeze was billowing through the pine trees. We still didn't know what to expect as we walked past the basic brown sign with the crisp white lettering, *Artist Point, Lower Falls*. Cote and I had not perused any Yellowstone brochure promoting what we were about to see; we had only Cousin Josh's highest recommendation from over a week ago to stop here if we found ourselves inside this incredible park. So, with only his words of wisdom to guide us, we hiked to the mysterious attraction.

We followed the stone pathway that led to a stone stairway. We took the steps up to the highest rock-laden platform, and then turned our gaze to the left. What we saw left us completely speechless.

Before our eyes stretched the most magnificent canyon I had ever seen. Carved in rich shades of caramel and glittering with sunlight, the show-stopping waterfall was full and spectacular. The water cascading over the high cliff fell like pure white gold, pounding the cavern below with power and presence. The view was raw, intense, stunning. Cote and I could do nothing more than stand and stare, as if cast under a spell of beauty beyond belief.

True to its name, an artist was on hand painting the picture-perfect scene. With his easel propped open and a half-painted canvas perched upon its wooden ledge, the artist was focused on recreating the canyon and its glorious waterfall with paintbrush and vibrant oils. I found myself feeling a little jealous of the man who sat upon his wooden stool oblivious to the people milling about him. He was completely caught up in the creativity of his art, unhurried and relaxed. I couldn't help but crave the freedom he was enjoying, to sit and breathe in the beauty, to work at a beloved craft for hours with no pressure to be someone or somewhere else—at least not for today.

I began to wonder where he was from, what his story was, and maybe even if he was on his own rite of passage. Cote and I snuck a few peeks over his shoulder, hoping he would find our curiosity flattering and turn to open up a line of casual conversation. To our disappointment, his attention remained unbroken. His gaze never left the hypnotic view. We gave up trying to break his stoic concentration and began snapping some digital pictures for our own keepsakes. I knew our camera would never hold, though, what our eyes were drinking in. The colors streaking the canyon walls were too distinct, rich, and dramatic to be reproduced on film. The cascading waterfall, though miles away, was too powerful and pounding for depiction on one-dimensional photo paper.

Taking pictures had become an important part of Cote's rite of passage, however. We knew these snapshots would aid our memory in the months and years to come; they would help us keep our journey alive, no matter how many days should come to pass. What's more, pictures would retell our story to future generations; they would become a vital part of our history, like treasured artifacts hidden within the layers of who we were at this time, at this place.

After several amazing minutes, Cote and I finally had to turn our backs on this spectacular view. With heavy hearts and weighted sighs, we retraced our steps to the parking lot. It was so hard to walk away, but the sun was inching across the western sky, slowly erasing the day. There was so much more for us to see and do. We knew we had to keep moving.

Back at the parking lot, we discovered yet another unexpected beauty—this time man-made. Sitting four cars down from our Ford Edge was a mint condition, retro-refurbished Volkswagen van—the kind I had longed to own for years. The exterior was painted 1970's yellow and sported a snow-white roof with matching bumpers. Curtains hung in all the back windows, completing the symbolic allure of peace, love, and all things happy. It was cool, yet calm; classy, but unique. The van epitomized all my vehicular dreams come true.

Cote and I walked around it with great admiration, failing to find one mark or dent. It oozed character; it dripped with charm.

"You should get one of these, Mom."

"Yeah. Right."

"What? Why not? You've always wanted one."

"Yeah, but wanting one doesn't mean I belong in one or can just go out and get one."

Cote and I gave the old girl a few more appreciative looks and then headed towards our car. We opened the doors to cool the interior and took swigs from our bottled water. Before we could get in, however, the owners of the VW returned.

They were easy to spot even from across the parking lot, for they matched the van perfectly. The two twenty-something-year olds, one male, one female, both sported longish hair and baggy clothes. He was unshaven; she was free of makeup. They were clean, but they walked with an air of earthy unconcern as to whether they would or wouldn't be by tomorrow.

"Mom, go talk to them."

"Yeah? And say what?"

"I don't know. How about, 'Wanna sell it?'"

"Uh, huh. Maybe they'd be interested in trading theirs for ours, right?"

"C'mon, Mom. What have you got to lose?"

Reminiscent of our conversation back along the shoreline of the Pacific Ocean, I knew the answer was, "Absolutely nothing." For reasons I couldn't put into words, I quickly grabbed a piece of paper from the car and jotted down my name and phone number. Then I folded the note to fit the palm of my hand as Cote and I ambled over.

"Hi," I offered first. "Great van."

"Thanks. She is great, isn't she?" the young man replied, as he looked upon his prized possession with warm admiration.

"How long have you had her?"

"Um, just over six years. I got her in Canton, Ohio."

Canton, Ohio! That's where my sister lives and has for over ten years. My mind raced with all the possibilities lost so long ago. "Canton, huh? Wow. That's where my sister lives."

"Yeah? It's a long ways away, isn't it?"

"Yes. Yes, it is. So she runs good?"

"Well, she does now. But not when I first got her. I had to fix her up a bit. Replaced the motor—twice. That was the biggest thing. But now she runs great, so it was totally worth it. I mean, look—she got us all the way out here to Yellowstone, right? So, I can't complain at all."

"Wow. And she's beautiful. You did a great job restoring her. So. Hmm, I don't suppose you've ever thought about selling her, have you?"

"Aw, naw. I don't think I could do that," he replied, with a soft, shy laugh.

"Yeah...I didn't think so." A few more seconds passed, while we all stood and stared at the yellow gem sitting before us. "But, I tell you what...just in case you ever change your mind, here's my name and number."

The young man's face broke into the biggest smile I'd ever seen, and he staggered just a bit as I placed the folded piece of paper into his open palm. He shook his head in disbelief, and laughed like a child surprised on Christmas morning. "No way! Really? Cool!"

"Yeah, it is cool. Well, okay then, I guess we better get going. Keep the number, you know—just in case you ever change your mind. It was nice meeting you both. Take care."

"Ha! Yeah. You too. Thanks!"

I was almost a little disappointed that he didn't throw at least one *"groovy"* our way before we departed. As Cote and I ducked inside our car, I stole a quick glance back over at the young man. He was still standing in the same spot, grinning from ear to ear, looking at the piece of paper in his hand.

Despite having struck out on my spontaneous offer, I couldn't help but smile, too. Truth be told, I don't know what I would have done had he agreed to make a deal. At least this way, though, I could still daydream of someday being the owner. We pulled away from the parking lot and as I watched the van get smaller and smaller in my rearview mirror, a famous song by Aerosmith floated to the surface of my mind. Before I knew it, I was humming along with the lyrics, "Dream on, dream on, dream on...dream until the dream comes true."

From Artist Point, Cote and I drove to the upper falls of the Yellowstone River. Though not quite as impressive as the 308-foot drop of the lower, this was still a worthwhile stop to make. We found ourselves standing on a rock platform that jutted precariously above the river's 110-foot drop, surprised by how close we could come to the rushing water. From this position, we could feel the power of the water as it pushed over the rocky ledge right beneath our feet. Its deafening roar filled our ears while the misty spray sent thousands of shimmering droplets into the air, tickling our exposed skin. A mini-rainbow danced upon the water's surface and showed up in almost every picture we took. This river moved forward with purpose and pride, grace and beauty. Looking down, I saw how the years of pounding water had shaped the very rock upon which I now stood, making it slick and smooth while uncovering a multitude of glorious layers hidden beneath.

With this thought in mind, I reflected on how the challenges in life often work in much the same manner. My own struggles had etched and carved and eroded the surface of my being. The forces of my past pushed against me—oftentimes without mercy. Yet they were the same forces that ending up molding me into someone I never thought I could be. I had been chipped, scraped, and scratched, but as a result, my true core had been uncovered. The process took time—lots of time. I had to wait for my jagged wounds to heal and smooth before I could see the good that had been revealed.

I believe this is true for all of us. We must be patient and forgiving in order to mend and let go. The difficulties we endure have the power to release the real beauty and strength we have hidden far beneath our gritty surfaces. And it is when our own truth is uncovered that we can finally see the truth and beauty in each other.

Yellowstone: Mount Washburn, 4:30 p.m.

Although you may not be able to reach the peak,
I will continue to try.
And when I get to the top of the mountain, for both of us,
I will fly.
~Quote written on poster board at the top of Mount Washburn

After leaving Artist Point, Cote and I turned the car towards Mount Washburn. This was to be our third and final destination inside Yellowstone. We intended to hike the 10,243' mountain and reach its peak before nightfall. However, just as life has a way of twisting and turning when you least expect it, we were spun off our course within minutes of leaving Artist Point—all because of a galloping horse and rider.

The two caught Cote's eye from the back corner of her passenger-side window just before they charged over the rugged ridge and out of sight. Cote immediately sucked in her breath, swiveled her head towards me, and started to beg, "Please, oh please, can we ride horses while we're here?"

"What? Cote, we don't have time. It's already 4:30. We still have to climb Mount Washburn and then drive out of Yellowstone so we can find a place to sleep tonight. It's too much. We just can't do everything."

"But riding horses would be the best! How about we just stay here tonight and then ride tomorrow?"

"We can't. There are no rooms left anywhere. Everything's booked up. I saw the sign this morning when we pulled in through the front gate. Cote, it's just not possible."

"But it looks like so much fun. C'mon, Mom. When we will get here again? If we don't do it now, we never will. Let's ride horses. Pleeeease!"

How is it that after years of saying no to my daughter as a persistent toddler and impulsive adolescent, I cannot seem to utter the word to this eighteen-year-old-version of Cote sitting next to me now? Against my better judgment, I pulled over and pulled out our Yellowstone map. Then I found the nearest horse corral.

I knew we were taking on too much. There was no way we could fit this all in and still leave Yellowstone before nightfall. Hopefully, I wouldn't have to be the one to break this news to Cote, however. With any luck, the clerk at the reservation counter would do it for me, by telling us the riding tours were finished for the day. Then we could move on as planned, without me having to be the bad guy.

"Hi. We'd like to book a couple of horses for an afternoon ride?"

"Sorry. The last group of the day just left. We won't go out again until tomorrow morning."

"Oh, okay. Well, then." I turned to Cote, ready to give up, but ran straight into the puppy dog eyes of my daughter. With half a heart, I rotated my body back towards the counter and choked out the following question. "Um, well, do you have any available rides first thing in the morning?"

"Ten o'clock has two spots open if you want them."

Now there were puppy dog eyes and a head nodding furiously beside me.

"Okay, put us down. Last name's Witt."

We left the corral with two riding reservations and a whole

new agenda. We wouldn't be leaving the park tonight. Somehow, somewhere, we'd have to find a place to sleep—and the only option I could see was the Ford Edge sitting in the dusty parking lot across from the ticket station.

"Whoo, hoo! Thanks, Mom!"

"Yeah? Well, don't be thanking me yet. We still have to climb Mount Washburn and now it looks like we'll be sleeping in the car tonight."

"C'mon. It's all part of the adventure, right?"

Yeah. All part of the adventure, my mind sighed.

The one part of this whole journey I wouldn't negotiate, however, was our safety. It was already late afternoon, and we still wanted to conquer the three-mile hike up Mount Washburn. My mind began to question if we had enough time to make the round-trip to the top and back before nightfall. Six miles would be no easy task, not with half of those spent hiking upward. One thing I was sure of—being caught after dark in the wilds of Yellowstone wouldn't be safe. At all.

As luck would have it, just as my questions began popping up, a Yellowstone Visitor's Center appeared around the next curve in the road. I pulled into the parking lot, relieved I could ask for some expert advice.

The ranger on duty was an older gentleman, white-haired, with a well-worn map of a face. His eyes seemed to hold an infinite amount of wisdom. I breathed a sigh of relief, confident he would have the answers we were searching for.

"Hi. We have a couple questions about hiking Mount Washburn. What's the latest time you would suggest for someone to begin a hike to the top?"

"Oh, I'd say by 4:30," he replied. Hesitantly, he added, "You don't want to be caught up there after dark."

"Four-thirty, eh? Hmm, it's almost that time now. Do you think we can still make it?"

"Well, I think so. Parking lot's not too far down the road. You should be all right," he offered, with a slight hint of uncertainty. Needless to say, his was not the voice of reassurance I had been hoping for.

Although we walked out of the Visitors' Center feeling less informed than when we walked in, Cote and I decided to take on Mount Washburn. We were here and now we were staying overnight. We had a few hours of daylight left, and we wanted to make the most of them. Whether or not we could reach the top of the mountain before nightfall would remain a mystery—that is, until we at least tried.

Cote and I hopped back into the car and within minutes, we were parked at the trailhead to Mount Washburn. After trading in our flip-flops for tennis shoes, Cote grabbed our camera and I retrieved a light backpack, throwing a water bottle inside. Although the initial incline looked a bit intimidating, we thought the trail would surely level off around the first bend, so with great enthusiasm and energy we started to climb.

Just a few steps into the hike we came face-to-face with a marmot nibbling on wildflowers along the edge of the footpath. We stopped to snap his picture and coo over his cuteness.

Turning our attention back to the trail, we rounded the first bend, only to be dumbfounded by what we saw. The path didn't level out at all. It continued on in the same direction—up. Already needing to catch our breath, Cote and I looked at each other in shock and exasperation. *What, exactly, have we gotten ourselves into?*

We weren't ready to give in, though. We dug in our heels and continued to climb. After a few switchbacks—zigzagging in a slow, methodical manner up the mountainside—Cote and I began brainstorming ways to outsmart the trail. In hopes of cutting our time in half, we decided to skip the next long, curving incline, and try scaling straight up instead—climbing from our lower section of trail to the barely visible, much higher one up the side of Mount Washburn.

Cote and I picked our way through rocks and low-hanging tree branches, scraping our hands and knees. Our legs burned by the time we conquered the sharp incline, and our attempt to save precious minutes proved futile. It took us just as long to catch our breath, huffing and puffing after our more strenuous exertion, than it did to follow each twist and turn of the gravel pathway.

We decided to return to the trail's switchback pattern—taking it slow but steady. Over the next hour, the only other hikers Cote and I met were all coming down the mountainside. Not one hiker passed us heading up. Each trekker greeted us with a small smile and a kind hello, and they all seemed confident in both step and direction. The exchanges were pleasant enough, but also raised that nagging notion in the back of my brain again. *Are we starting this hike too late?*

About halfway up the mountain, the rocky landscape gave way to a beautiful wooded area, stretching back into a green-black cavern. The trees grew thick, and the shade was incredibly inviting against the heat of the late-afternoon sun and our constant climbing. Cote and I rested on a stump, scanning the dark leafy edges hoping to spot more forest creatures enjoying a snack of wildflowers. To our delight, an immature elk moseyed by minutes later, rustling a few branches in its wake and munching lazily on the leaves of some low-hanging limbs.

As the beautiful animal drifted into the dense brush, Cote and I stood. Without thinking we took a few steps to follow it. Suddenly, a loud snorting and stomping sound came from the darkened interior, snapping us back into reality. We turned and sprinted towards the marked path and hightailed it up the mountain trail. For several seconds, we kept running, nervously looking over our shoulders, until we finally had to stop and catch our breath. It had been a stupid and careless moment. Cote and I had forgotten just how wild Yellowstone could be.

"Holy cow, Mom! What was that?"

"I don't know, Cote. I have no idea."

"Do you think we should keep going?"

"Yeah, I think we're okay."

"That was freaky."

"Yes, yes, it was. We better stick to the trail. And we better keep moving or we're not going to make it to the top. It's already six o'clock."

"How much longer before it gets dark?"

"I don't know but why don't we do this: let's promise that if we're not at the top by seven o'clock, we'll turn around, no matter where we are, and head back down. Its already been an hour and a half, and I'm not sure how far up we've even gone."

"Okay. Sounds good."

So, with Yellowstone as our witness, Cote and I pinkie promised each other right then and there to end our ascent in an hour. We didn't know how far we'd get, or if we'd even see the top of Mount Washburn before our time was up, but so far, the climb had been exciting and worth the effort. We'd keep going until our last second ran out.

At twenty minutes to seven, we rounded yet another switchback, and finally the majestic peak of Mount Washburn came into view. We stopped short, blinking in disbelief. The crown of our pilgrimage was still a good distance away but just to have it within sight renewed our energy.

Cote and I picked up our pace, as much as we could, for the terrain was still nearly vertical and very taxing. Our legs were sore and tired, yet we pressed forward, placing one foot determinedly in front of the other.

To our amazement—almost as if our promise had been heard by the heavens above—we reached the top of Mount Washburn at exactly 7:00 p.m. Cote and I twirled 360 degrees with the wind whipping against our outstretched arms, the cool air filling our lungs. Not another soul was in sight. We had the mountaintop all to ourselves. The panoramic view was incredible. Spinning around, we felt as if we were flying on top of the world. Our bodies reenergized as our spirits circled and soared.

After several minutes of enjoying the view and our accomplishment, Cote and I ventured inside the lookout station. In front of a huge plate-glass window overlooking the expansive mountain range, we found a book perched on display. Its pages were filled with the names of those who had also conquered Mount Washburn. They had come from all across the country and all over the globe. With a dose of thankfulness and a smidgen of pride, Cote and I added our own names to the signature book. We left our mark of victory, forever pressed between the pages of those who had already been here and those who would someday come.

We knew we couldn't stay much longer. The clock was still ticking, and it had taken us two and a half hours to climb up here. Going back down would surely be much faster, but we still had three full miles to cover before nightfall. Cote and I took one last look around the peak and then began our descent.

We started by half jogging-half skipping down the gravel path, and covered a good portion of ground fairly quickly. The terrain was nothing new at this point, but the setting sun was softening the edges of the landscape, casting a feathery hue upon every bush, tree, and rock. We slowed our gait for a moment, to invite the peace and quiet to seep into our skin. It was then that an unexpected and innocent question led to one of our most amazing mother-daughter conversations yet.

"Mom, how do you know whether you're making the right choices in life?"

At eighteen-years-old, we both knew Cote would soon be facing some important life-changing decisions. What I didn't know was that she was struggling already with these questions and the potential routes her life would take. The dialogue that opened up between us was deep and honest and at times, difficult. She shared her worries about the consequences of making wrong choices, as well as how uncertain and ill-equipped she felt at times to decide at all.

I offered her the best advice I could but then reminded her that ultimately it was up to her to decide what was right and what was true, for the young woman she was now, and for the woman she hoped to someday become.

Our conversation continued as we hiked the rest of the way down Mount Washburn. We expanded our discussion to include the life choices that would arise fifteen, twenty, and even twenty-five years from now. We delved into the topic of marriage and what it means to find the right person.

"Cote, I hope you never regret any events that happen to you in life, because those have the power to shape you into a strong and capable person," I shared.

From there we dipped into the idea of life being a journey of discovery—of finding out who we are along the way and who we want to become. "The tricky part is to not be afraid of being that person once you've found her," I said. "Especially when you're in the company of others."

We spoke of love and loss, and the struggle to recover one's footing after being knocked off center. We talked about the differences between compromising and conceding, and how important it is to make choices that lead to personal growth and inner peace. We acknowledged that we would face fear at times, but I encouraged her to be strong enough not let it get in the way of becoming who she wanted to be.

In all of these conversations, the mother bird in me could see my baby chick teetering on the scary edge of life's unknowns. Cote was strong, yet uncertain; excited, yet hesitant. She was stretching and flexing her wings right before my very eyes. I knew the day was quickly approaching, when she would trust those wings enough to fly.

It was nine o'clock by the time we reached the base of the mountain. We were physically exhausted. Our legs hurt and our feet ached. Our minds, however, rested in a soft, peaceful, connected place. We crawled inside the Ford Edge and let the leather seats cushion and cradle our worn-out bodies for a few blissful moments. Night was falling fast, and we were in need of a place to sleep, but the mountain behind us now held priceless and personal memories, memories that made it hard for me to put the car in gear to go. What's more, pieces of our hearts had been scattered along that three-mile, winding trail as well. We had left them exposed and unattended. As I closed my eyes for a few minutes, I realized this thought didn't worry me. I knew Mount Washburn could be trusted. I was confident the mighty mountain would gather up the precious pieces we'd left behind and keep them safe for us forever.

Yellowstone: Staying Overnight

~Sunsets~
Colors of purple and pink, As it slowly must sink.
God gave them for humans to treasure.
And I do.
~Jolene Fischer, Poem written at age 9, 1975

"The colors of a sunset, are never truly gone.
They rest inside the watching soul, throughout the whole
night long.
And when the light returns again, to dry the morning dew,
I promise to be mindful still, and begin the day anew."
~Jolene Witt, Rite of Passage journal entry, Day 10

Cote and I pulled away from Mount Washburn, feeling solemn but focused. It was time to find a place to spend the night.

The sun had long since set, and only a few remaining tentacles of light still struggled for grip along the distant horizon. The mountain peaks had disappeared with the sun. The meadows were slipping into soft oblivion. Soon everything would be swallowed in darkness, and there would be no street lamp flipped on to light our way. I drove feverishly to find the best place to park before everything faded to black.

We passed several scenic lookouts, slowing down long enough to debate the pros and cons of each one: location, size, and view all being considered. We finally found one that had everything we were looking for. It consisted of a small half-circle turn-out, beautifully situated above a sunken valley. It faced east, with mountains softly filling in the farthest edges of the horizon. We could point our car straight towards the picturesque view, and in the morning when the sun came up, its warm rays would overtake the peaks and spread across the meadow, eventually seeping through our waiting windshield. This, we decided, would be the perfect place to be awakened by the magic of Yellowstone.

We pulled in and immediately began to repack the car. Cote and I had to clear space in the backseat so that we could lay the front seats as flat as possible for sleeping. We tossed all our everyday gear inside the back hatch and grabbed pillows, blankets, books, and flashlights. We brushed our teeth using bottled water and washed our faces with disposable cleansing cloths. We changed into flannel pants and fresh T-shirts, then climbed back into the Edge's front seats to see just how comfortable our makeshift "beds" would be.

Excitement overrode any other thought for a while. We weren't ready to close our eyes just yet, so Cote and I talked about our day, the challenges we had faced, the fun we had shared. We revealed our hopes for tomorrow and fantasized about what adventures another new day in Yellowstone might bring. Night had now fully arrived, but the possibility of one or two more passing cars kept us from using the "outside facilities" just yet. We wanted to make sure the coast was clear before we completed that final bedtime ritual.

It was then that a startling idea popped inside my head: *What if it's against the law for us to park overnight in Yellowstone?*

"Cote. Holy cow. What if this isn't legal?"

"What? What are you talking about?"

"Parking overnight," I said. "What if we're not supposed to do this?"

"What? Why? We're not hurting anything."

"I know that, but I bet we're not supposed to. Think about it. If parking overnight was legal, everybody would do it. I mean, there would be people all over the place. And what a mess *that* would be. There'd be all kinds of trash left behind. Oh, my gosh. I bet this isn't allowed."

I twisted in my seat and rummaged through the storage compartment of my driver-side door, pulling out the Yellowstone Visitor's Guide I had stuffed in there first thing this morning when we paid at the gate. Flipping through its pages, I found what I was looking for: all the "Do's and Don'ts" while visiting this national park.

Rule #8 -- Overnight Vehicular Parking Is Not Permitted

And here we were. Sitting ducks. Out in the open, proudly parked for all to see.

Now what?

I yanked my seat back to its upright position and turned the engine over. One thing was for sure—we couldn't stay here. Where could we go, though? All the lodges and campgrounds were full, and it would take too long to drive all the way out of the park tonight, only to drive all the way back in tomorrow morning. We had no choice. We needed a place to *hide*.

Driving was now dangerous; all visibility was stripped down to only the width and length of our headlight beams. Twists and turns that had been leisurely and gentle just hours ago, were now menacing and intimidating. Walls of rock appeared suddenly without warning, narrowing the road and pushing me to the outer edge. I gripped the steering wheel, trying to keep both the car and my breathing under control.

Around one particularly sharp curve, our headlights caught the eyes and surprise of a red-tail fox crossing the road. Instinctively, I took my foot off the gas, and he scurried into the brush unharmed. Coming upon the unexpected nocturnal animal reminded me of the need to be cautious for him and any others that might be moving about as I tried to navigate these roads. My anxiety kicked up another notch. The tension in my shoulders tightened. I had no idea where we were or where we were going, but the only places we'd seen to pull over were lookout points in plain sight, and those wouldn't do.

Ten minutes later we came upon a deserted service drive leading to a small picnic area. With a sigh of relief, I took the turn-off leaving the main road behind us. Driving through the short tunnel of trees, the road forked again and to our right sat a few wooden picnic tables flanking a small circular parking lot. The area was secluded and empty and pitch-black. It was perfect. I tucked our car as far back into the pine-tree line as I could, put it in park, and cut the lights.

The night swallowed us whole.

Initially it was unnerving to be sitting in such total and complete darkness. However, since we couldn't see a thing inside or outside our car, I knew this meant our jet-black Ford Edge couldn't be seen, either. And that's exactly what we needed.

A hoot owl screeched his objection about our arrival, sending shivers down Cote's arms and up my spine. This was going to be one long and interesting night, no doubt. Visions of bears, wolves, and other not-so-friendly animals began creeping into my imagination. For the past thirty minutes, all I wanted was for us to find a place of total isolation—completely hidden from sight and cut off from civilization. Now that we had exactly what I'd hoped for, I felt in many ways more exposed and vulnerable than ever before.

Cote and I grabbed two blankets and our books. We thought if we read for a while, we'd relax and grow too tired to worry about what might be lurking in the shadows. Then, hopefully, we would fall into an idyllic and oblivious night of sleep. Reading posed another problem, however. Flipping on our book lights meant possibly drawing unwanted attention. So Cote and I decided to throw the covers over our heads to block their silvery glow.

Within minutes we both reemerged, throwing our blankets aside, and having to admit we'd reread the same page over and over again. Our minds were refusing to focus and let go of our desolate and untamed location. We closed our books and decided to pray for sleep, instead. Before we could do that, however, there was one final detail that needed to be addressed.

The object of our dilemma sat on the other side of the picnic area, less than fifty yards away. Nevertheless, the wooden outhouse might as well have been on top of Mount Washburn. There was no way we were going over there, no way we would venture that far from the safety of our car. Who knew what creature was watching us from the wood-line, waiting for us to make one stupid mistake? Anything could be *out* there...or come to think of it...*in* there.

"So, what do we do?"

"Well, Cote, I think I'm going to quietly open my door, pee right here beside the car, and then jump back in."

"Okay. Sounds good to me."

I can't remember ever feeling so relieved and anxious at the same time, but with our final business of the day taken care of,

Cote and I settled in for what remained of the night.

Sleep for me was fitful at best and terribly short-lived. Throughout the night, I lost count of how many times I woke up because my spine was folded into an odd origami-shape and my legs were twisted like pretzels. At some point the moon broke free of the clouds and shone full and bright through our front windshield and into my face, fooling me into believing morning had arrived. Cote, however, slept soundly right beside me. Being so much younger and more flexible, her body allowed itself to curl, squish, and contort into all different shapes and sizes. Not once did she awaken to complain of a twinge, a cramp, or an ache.

At 5:45 the next morning, I gave up my pursuit for more sleep. I unfolded my body one last time, stretched my legs, and pulled my seat back to its upright position. During the past two hours, the cold air outside had crept its way inside our car, dropping the interior temperature to the point where our blankets were no longer enough. Cote stirred just as I reached for the ignition key. Still in a sleep-like trance, she asked me to turn on the heat. I did just that, and then one better: I punched the button for her seat-warmer. With the engine humming, Cote curled her body towards the passenger-side door, bunched herself into a blanket-covered ball, and drifted back into her dreams.

Darkness still surrounded us, solid and black, but I had a plan of action in my head. The first streaks of sunrise would soon be breaking the horizon, and I wanted Cote to wake up where we had originally intended to spend the night—the spot overlooking the meadow with the mountains in the distance. It would take some careful navigating to get us there, but that's where my heart was telling me to go.

Fifteen minutes later, I found it. Pulling the car over, I took a deep breath, exhaling a prayer of thanks. We were here and we were safe. We had survived our homeless night in Yellowstone.

The sky to the east began to warm with color, so I gently shook Cote awake. I didn't want her to miss even a single minute of the magic that was coming. She stretched her body and blinked the sleep from her eyes in disbelief. Together we watched the sun slowly rise above the mountaintop, ushering in a gorgeous new day. It was peaceful, powerful, and spiritual—everything I had hoped it would be.

I couldn't think of a better time or place to give my daughter her next rite of passage letter. I pulled it from my bag and slipped it silently into her open hands.

Day 11: Yellowstone to Billings, Montana, 408 miles

Oh, give me a home.
Where the buffalo roam.
And the deer and the antelope play.
-American Folk Song

The sun broke full upon our majestic mountain. While its dazzling rays warmed our morning sky, Cote snuggled back down beneath her blanket and returned to that distant world of sleep. I was fine with her decision. Having her close her eyes and feel safe enough to trust that I would watch over her—if only for a few more hours—felt good. We had shared the sunrise, and Cote had read today's letter. Now I had a few quiet moments to myself.

I used the time to meditate and pray, allowing my mind to pick through the long list of items I had to be grateful for. I gave thanks for the morning vista, for the precious time Cote and I would have to spend together today, and for our protection from all things harmful during the night. It felt good to be silent, mindful, and present.

As I started the car back up, I couldn't help but think how a hot cup of coffee would taste heavenly right then. I knew finding one, however, would be nothing short of a small miracle.

We had been homeless all-night and it wasn't even seven o'clock yet. Mountains, and prairies, and valleys stretched for miles in every direction, and all the visitors' centers were still closed. My chances of scoring a hot cup of coffee this early in the morning were slim to none.

Nevertheless, I felt a little like Dorothy in the Wizard of Oz as I pulled the car away from the lookout point. I had a magical road full of adventure before me. Though it wasn't made of brick, so far *Yellow-stone* had proven to be just as full of sweet surprises and unexpected delights as Dorothy had found on her journey to Oz. It couldn't hurt to start driving and see where my fairy-tale path would take me.

Thirty minutes later, I pulled into the legendary Theodore Roosevelt Lodge and Riding Stable. This was where we were to saddle up and begin our horseback riding, but not until ten o'clock.

The place was quiet and subtle, warm with a rustic flair. Tiny log cabins dotted the perimeter of the circular drive, and hitching posts designated parking spots. Despite the large number of vehicles, I didn't see one person moving about. The place had all the makings of a deserted ghost town.

I decided to leave Sleeping Beauty locked inside the Edge while I tried the door to the main lodge and dining hall. I wasn't sure they'd even be open this early, but I figured there was no harm in trying to find out. I climbed the wooden planks and walked across the well-worn porch. The rocking chairs to my right were empty and inviting, swaying slightly in the soft morning breeze. I reached for the handle of the large oak door, thinking it wouldn't budge under my pull. However, surprisingly, it sprang free.

The room before me was enormous and full of more wood: paneled walls, a timber-framed ceiling, heavy oak tables and chairs, and a scuffed hardwood floor. Three young workers were quietly setting up for what appeared to be a very large anticipated breakfast crowd. Gingerly, I stepped inside, feeling every bit an imposter, a fraud upon their premises.

Will the staff know that I'm not a registered guest? That I'm really a rule-breaker? An overnight stowaway?

Before I could turn in shame, the smell of freshly brewed coffee stopped my self-defeating thoughts. The aroma was as warm and welcoming as the morning sun had been an hour ago. Here was my great and magical Oz! To my right stood corrals of coffeepots upon a table by the front window. Had the room been empty of wait staff, I would have made a beeline for the prized beverage. As it was, however, my entrance had caught the attention of an elderly cowboy across the expansive room. He was smiling at me from behind his reservation counter.

I timidly smiled back, which resulted in him enthusiastically waving me over. Taking a deep breath, I crossed the space between us. I was nervous to speak or even make eye contact, afraid I'd give my secret away. His face was nothing but relaxed and eager, though, and he didn't appear shocked at all by my early-morning arrival. He simply asked if he could help me.

"Um, yes. I know I'm early, but is this where I confirm reservations for horseback riding?"

"Yes, ma'am, you're in the right place. Let me give you the paperwork to fill out, and I'll just pull up the rest of your information in our computer system." He turned to his electronic keyboard.

"What's your name and where are you staying inside Yellowstone?"

"Um, last name's Witt, and well, um, we're not staying here. My daughter and I stopped at the Canyon Corral yesterday and spoke to someone there about booking a ride for this morning."

"Okay. Well, let me see if I can find your reservation then. Hmm...Yep, here you are. I have two riders for Witt scheduled for ten o'clock this morning."

"Yes, that's right. That's us. Do I pay for it now?"

"Yep, then you'll be all set. Plan on being at the stable across the yard about fifteen minutes before your ride begins."

"All right. Thank you for your help."

I paid for our passes and though I wasn't sure I should press my luck, I couldn't stop myself from asking one more question. "Um...by the way...could I buy a cup of coffee over there? It smells so good and I could really use some."

"Oh, absolutely! But it's free. Just help yourself."

"But, I'm not a guest here."

"That's no problem. Just get yourself some. It's on the house."

"Thank you! Thank you very much."

I couldn't believe how this day was unfolding. It wasn't even eight o'clock, and already so much had happened. My daughter and I had shared a beautiful sunrise together inside a gorgeous national park. I had spent an hour meditating and quietly driving through some incredible landscapes. I now had a cup of steaming hot coffee in my hands and in about two hours, Cote and I would be riding horses across an open prairie.

Could our trip get any better?

The bright sun had me squinting when I stepped back outside. Through the windshield, I could see Cote was still fast asleep. With plenty of time to play, I slid back into the car and found Lamar Valley on our handy-dandy Yellowstone map. The brochure said this area held the best opportunity for spotting wildlife, if you were an early-morning riser.

Let's go see what we can find, I thought.

Fifteen minutes later, I rounded a curve in the road and spotted a mountain goat sunning himself high on a ridge to our left. I woke Cote up, and we used our binoculars to study the finer details of his features—his soft gray fur, his calm, cool eyes. It was a far-off and simple sighting, yet we were excited to see something so wild and free in its natural habitat. Little did we know that our animal encounters were going to become up-close and personal around the very next bend.

Bison filled the countryside by the hundreds. They were everywhere, in every direction. There was buffalo in the road blocking our path, while others stood their ground along the grassy shoulder. Many more were grazing in the distant fields. It looked like a scene right out of the movie *Dances with Wolves*.

The magnificent creatures were poised and picture-perfect. We could see the breath of the ones right next to us and hear their snorts as they moved about. With our vehicle giving us a false sense of safety, we studied the beasts in great detail. Thick woolly coats, large brown eyes, hunched, massive backs. The adults were bulky but graceful, and despite their powerful bodies, they seemed gentle as they foraged for their breakfast. The babies were timid and uncertain. They nuzzled close to their mothers for protection and security.

I was wowed by their presence, but even more so at their willingness to share their space. Here we were intruding upon their territory, entering their habitat. We were uninvited guests, yet we were allowed to linger and roam alongside them. The minutes slipped by. Cote and I found ourselves slowing to match the peacefulness of their pace. Life in this lane of leisure was rich with beauty. These animals were nothing short of poetry in motion.

Cote and I drove through Lamar Valley, stopping every so

often for more pictures, more slowed, breathable moments. By the time our two hours were up, we'd seen several elks, a coyote, two small packs of pronghorns, and an osprey soaring overhead with a prized fish in his talons. We returned to the Teddy Roosevelt Riding Stable energized and ready to scout for more wild animals, this time on horseback.

Our trail guides met us at the stables fifteen minutes before the hour. We exchanged quick introductions and then they gave us a few simple instructions. Afterwards, my fearless daughter went straight to her horse, Frito, and flung herself onto his back. Her confidence impressed me, as I had never been that brave or bold around horses. Cautiously approaching my designated steed, Russell, I offered my open hand and gently patted his neck, hoping my gestures would make us instant friends. *Friends don't throw friends,* I thought.

Cote shook her head at me, and chuckled lightly from her solid equestrian perch. Then she excitedly began to recall the horse and rider she had seen the day before, the way the two had galloped as one across the hillside.

"I can't wait to do that."

"Just be careful, Cote."

"Oh, Mom, relax. This is going to be fun!"

When all ten riders in our group were saddled up, we set off single file from the stable towards the wide-open prairie across the road. We had an hour of western frontier at our hooves, and we couldn't wait to start exploring John Wayne-style.

It didn't take long for us to realize that no galloping was going to take place. Cantering and trotting were out of the question, too. Our horses were trained to move at one speed only—slow. I'm sure this was for liability reasons, but it was still a great disappointment to Cote. She had so been looking forward to riding fast and fiercely across the wide-open fields of Yellowstone.

Our guides, Tracy, Billie, and Mike, made our adventure worthwhile, though. They filled our riding time with fascinating stories and little-known facts about Yellowstone. They told us how the horses (over a hundred throughout the national park), were turned loose every winter to fend for themselves upon the open prairies of Montana. There, the animals would have to survive the harshest of seasons alone. Every spring, ranchers would ride out to round up the horses and bring them back to the riding stables inside Yellowstone. Here, they would be corralled once again to serve the summer tourists who would arrive with the warmer weather.

My thoughts began to wander in a strange direction after hearing this interesting bit of information. I wondered if living through such drastic and contradictory conditions twice a year was confusing for the horses. Were they lost and lonely during the winter, or wildly independent and carefree? Did they crave the security of summer and knowing where their next meal was coming from? Or did they find this corralled and controlled environment mind-numbing and frustrating? Did they relish the challenge of winter or prefer the stability of summer?

Tracy shared the most intriguing story while we rode the trails through Yellowstone. She told us the tale of the great fire of 1988, the one that burned almost 800,000 acres of the national park, destroying a little more than thirty percent of its 2.2 million.

Several fires raged out of control that summer due to drought and high winds, she said, but a cigarette carelessly tossed in the state of Idaho had ignited this one. The flame from that spark grew into a maddening, out-of-control inferno. It blazed its way to the sacred grounds of Yellowstone, obliterating everything in its path. I thought about the firefighters who fought those raging flames and how helpless they must have felt back then. Tracy told us their efforts seemed minuscule and futile, until the unthinkable happened.

On September 11, 1988, it started to snow. Apparently, it wasn't unheard-of to have a snowstorm in September, but this particular squall showed up at just the right time and in the location where it was needed the most. The fires had drawn dangerously close to the Theodore Roosevelt Lodge and Riding Stable, the one we had just left an hour ago.

It looked as if this historical site would soon be the next victim of the horrible inferno. However, a quarter-inch of snow followed by several days of rain put a stop to the fire's destruction. The flames that had been raging out of control for months were finally and fully extinguished. Millions of acres inside Yellowstone National Park had been saved by what many had thought to be a miracle.

Moments later, as when we rode back towards the riding stables, we could see where the trees had been charred on the backside of the mountain behind the Teddy Roosevelt Lodge. It was heartbreaking to see the devastation and loss. Through the scars, however, small shoots of green were fighting to take hold. Rebirth was happening in this corner of Yellowstone, giving clear signs of hope and new life to all those fortunate enough to visit and take witness.

With our ride coming to an end, Cote and I could feel our time in Yellowstone coming to an end, as well. We dismounted our trusted horses and said our good-byes. It was time to head for the North Gate and connect with Route 89. Montana was waiting for us there, along with I-90 East—the road which would eventually lead us home. Even though we still had more than 1,500 miles to cover, I could feel the very tangible end of Cote's rite of passage approaching. Squinting against the sun, I could almost see it on the distant horizon.

At Yellowstone's North Gate, Cote and I pulled the car over and snapped one final picture of this incredible place, with all its wildlife and untamed spirit. We had found freedom and adventure inside this massive nature-filled sanctuary. We had climbed to the top of a mountain and delved into the very core of our souls. Yellowstone held beauty and grace. It was a land full of legends and stories, told and retold. As I watched the stone gates disappear in my rearview mirror, I realized Cote and I now carried some of those stories with us, as well. And what an honor it would be to share those tales with others.

Day 12: Billings, Montana to Chamberlain, South Dakota, 660 miles

Eastbound and down, loaded up and truckin'.
We gonna do what they say can't be done.
~ Jerry Reed, *Smokey and the Bandit,* 1977

Today Cote and I put the hammer down and gave the road all we had. By the time we pulled over for the night, Yellowstone was over six hundred miles behind us.

This is not to say, however, that we were in a hurry to get home. We still had a lot of ground to cover and several more adventures to look forward to. Cote's rite of passage was still in full swing. Nevertheless, when we awoke this morning, we had to face a very hard truth—this was our twelfth day gone from home and we had just spent the past twenty-seven hours traipsing through Yellowstone. It was time for us to log some serious miles. So we loaded up the car and turned our eyes eastward.

We set our sights on Mount Rushmore and the Black Hills of South Dakota. I hadn't been to this area in more than thirty years, not since I was a young girl riding in the backseat of my parents' Oldsmobile. I tried to recall some of my memories of Mount Rushmore but most of the images that surfaced were sketchy at best.

Only two stood out in sharp enough detail to share with Cote: the intense heat and a waist-high concrete wall. It was extremely hot the day my parents and I visited Mount Rushmore back in 1978—a very sweltering, melting kind of hot. I remember standing in the full sun on a concrete platform in front of a concrete barricade. The four famous faces had been impressive to behold but under the heat of the blazing sun, it was all I could do to keep the sweat from burning my eyes.

What I didn't remember was how far Mount Rushmore was from the expressway.

We exited the highway at Rapid City, South Dakota and turned onto a two-lane road, where we were met by a sign stating it would take us twenty-seven miles to reach our destination.

What?! Twenty-seven miles? One-way?! How could I have not known that?!

My original thought of this being a quick easy-off, easy-on, stop-and-look tourist attraction flew out the window. Now Cote and I had a three-hour time-consuming adventure ahead of us, which was too late to avoid. We were this close after all. We might as well make the drive to see the national landmark.

It was early afternoon when Cote and I pulled into the parking lot. By then our car's thermostat registered a temperature of one hundred degrees outside. We stepped from our vehicle into the heat, and then climbed the seven concrete steps to make our way across the concrete courtyard—all without any shade or protection from the sun's intensive rays. We passed through a stoic row of state flags, London Bridge style, stopping only long enough to locate Michigan's banner. Finally, Cote and I approached the waist-high wall that had been cemented into my childhood memories.

Mount Rushmore loomed high on the mountain before us, huge and bold. The faces of the four historic presidents were still a sight to see after all these years; the remarkable craftsmanship definitely a work of carved art. However, after two very short minutes, Cote and I had to confess that we were slightly bored and ready to go.

Maybe it was the heat pushing us to leave. Or possibly, it was the touristy feeling of the plaza. Whatever it was, Cote and I couldn't deny we were ready to move on. Later that evening, when I had a chance to reflect upon our day, I think what bothered us the most was the contrast in landscapes we had experienced in just a short twenty-four-hour period. Standing in front of the colossal man-carved Mount Rushmore, Cote and I couldn't help but subconsciously compare it to the untouched natural beauty of Yellowstone. The two were polar opposites. Yellowstone had touched our hearts, had seeped into our souls. Mount Rushmore, on the other hand, seemed a bit too cold, a little too artificial in its design.

"Huh," I said, squinting against the sun. "So, what do you think?"

"It's okay, I guess."

"Yeah." A moment of silence passed. "Well, are you ready to go?"

"Yep, ready when you are."

With those words, Cote and I turned away from this national icon and headed back to our car. We did stop long enough to read a few of the historical facts etched into the concrete columns on our way out, as a means of paying respect and tribute to those who dedicated their lives to this great endeavor. Undeniably, Mount Rushmore was a grand undertaking and a source of national pride and accomplishment. Those who built it should be acknowledged, honored, and always remembered.

As we reached the exit to the parking lot, Cote and I were faced with yet another last-minute decision on her rite of passage. Should we make a beeline back for I-90 East, concentrating our efforts to make up for lost time? Or should we keep going deeper into the black hills of South Dakota and visit one more monument—the one devoted to the legendary Native American warrior, Crazy Horse?

"Let's go see it, Mom."

"But, Cote, it's seventeen more miles out of our way. It will be late by the time we start heading east again."

"So what? We're right here. If we don't go now, we might never get back this way again."

Once again, I had no way to argue with her logic, especially considering that thirty years had passed since I last walked these hills. In reality, it could take another thirty before my daughter came here again—and by then, I might not be around to hear about it. Turning the car in the opposite direction of the highway, I pushed all goal-oriented thinking aside and allowed the call of adventure to lead us where it willed.

Seventeen curving miles later, we arrived. I hardly recognized the place. The grounds of Crazy Horse had changed dramatically since 1978. Thirty years ago there was very little to see, just a short dirt driveway, leading to a ram-shackled visitors' center, and a mountain sculpture that was crude and unobstructed. Crazy Horse consisted only of a rough cutting of rock, a shaved ninety-degree ledge that would someday become the arm of the great Native American pointing towards the distant horizon. This was all my memory could recall.

Now, as Cote and I drove up the paved entranceway, Crazy Horse was blocked from our view by big, bold buildings of various shapes and sizes. The visitors' center was a huge and beautiful timber-framed building with large plate-glass windows. There was a souvenir-stuffed gift shop, a full-service sit-down restaurant, an open-air viewing deck, and a larger than life Native American museum. People were milling all over the grounds, sipping drinks, reading pamphlets, enjoying the day. My excitement level jumped three notches when I realized what all this must mean: the work to bring Crazy Horse to "life" must be over!

I could hardly believe that after thirty years, I was going to get to see the finished masterpiece. The jagged images from my childhood would be replaced today by a great monument, fully carved and completed, and I was going to be one of those people lucky enough to have witnessed the before and after.

Walking out to the viewing deck, I couldn't have been more wrong. Crazy Horse was nowhere near being finished—not even close.

I quickly scanned the pamphlet we'd been handed at the front door, and learned the monument didn't even have a projected completion date.

Crazy Horse was started in 1948 as a nonprofit undertaking. It was determined back then that the entire memorial would be funded only through the goodwill donations of those willing to give. No federal monies would ever be accepted to help pay for its carving. These policies were set in place in order to maintain the validity and integrity of the project. Thus, progress was slow. Very slow. Money, weather, and mountain engineering, all presented enormous challenges—and several severe setbacks.

This is not to say, though, that Cote and I weren't moved by the mountain before us. Crazy Horse's arm was still one long, straight, horizontal ledge with no defining detail, and the stallion upon which the North American warrior would someday ride had no shape or form as of yet. Nevertheless, the monument did have one major and poignant finished feature. Crazy Horse had a face—a solid, profound, and affecting face, with eyes that provoked a prickling of tears in my own. Cut slowly over the past thirty years with great care and determination, the coarse rock on this lonely mountainside had been transformed, and the face that emerged reflected hardship and heartache, along with hope and perseverance.

Cote and I took our time on the observation deck, and then we explored the rest of the grounds, including the massive museum. Here, history came alive in a very silent and humbling way. The pinewood-covered walls whispered of pain and hurt inflicted long ago, yet there was an air of forgiveness and healing, as well. We felt honored to be standing here; honored to look, touch, and remember these lessons from history.

We gazed through glass showcases at Native American artifacts made from leather and beads, wood and stone. We ducked inside an authentic tipi and we stopped to read the many personal stories and historical accounts on display. When we came to a rock box filled with stones collected from high atop Crazy Horse Mountain, Cote and I each selected a special one and made a donation to the cause.

Exploring these grounds had a profound effect upon us. Instead of being in a hurry to return to the highway and resume our journey, we now felt a need to slow down, to pause, and to remember.

As we lingered over the artifacts, Cote began to speak of her own Native American heritage. Her great-great-great grandmother on her father's side was a full-blooded member of the Pottawatomie tribe. Here, in the Black Hills of South Dakota, a spark had been ignited inside my daughter to research deeper into the history of her ancestors when we returned home. Strange as it may seem, Cote and I, both felt a stronger connection here than we did gazing at our American presidents just seventeen miles up the road.

When we finally left Crazy Horse, I couldn't help but remember the excitement I'd felt when we first pulled in, thinking I was going to see the finished monument. Now while driving away, I found myself appreciating the slow and steady process taking place. Crazy Horse was coming to life in its own time and in its own space. By this course of action, it was retaining its own sense of truth and authenticity. *How often do we strive to do just the opposite, though, in our own daily living?* I asked myself.

Most of us can honestly say that we've been guilty of rushing our lives at times. We are anxious to see the fruits of our labor. We want quick and profitable results. The sad part is that when we narrow our focus to only the prize at the end of the finish line, we lose out on the magic of the journey required to get us there.

Real life is about the stories being written in the smaller moments of the everyday. The essence of our lives comes more from the times we tend to overlook than from those we think of as most crucial. When I took one last look back at Crazy Horse, I thought of all the people who have and who are dedicating their lives to making this work of art a reality. Many of them will never see the carving to its completion. Yet they work on, knowing that they are making a difference. They are creating a masterpiece. They are telling a story—one that needs to be told. Through their sweat and tears, their joy and determination, they must hold on to a hope that someday a future generation will stand before this great mountain in both awe and appreciation.

Each of us, to some degree, has a story to tell. We all sweat and cry. We all laugh and try to push on—every day, in our own way. We fight our battles and face our challenges, to reach our triumphs and overcome our setbacks. Most of us hope to make a difference, big or small, in the lives of those we touch, of those we love. The untold stories written deep inside our hearts need to be shared. We should try to carve them into our own little piece of mountainside, for when we do, we may just give hope to others who are searching. And we may discover strength in ourselves in return. We stand to add dimension, depth, and detail to our daily lives. My wish for Cote is that she will always see the value in sharing her life story as it unfolds. I hope she'll recognize the purpose and passion of her journey, and I pray she will never stop noticing the magical moments along the way.

Cote and I didn't immediately skirt back to Interstate 90 after leaving Crazy Horse. Instead, we took a remote route that led us through the heart of South Dakota's infamous Badlands. The road we chose was deserted, dry, and desolate. The landscape was barren, eerie, and yet captivatingly beautiful in its own simple and monochromatic way. This road was vastly different from any road we'd traveled so far. We drove for miles through a land that time itself seemed to have forgotten.

At nine o'clock in the evening, we pulled into Chamberlain, South Dakota and booked a room at the Super 8 Motel. Cote and I were exhausted but happy with how we had spent our day. We ordered a small pizza from a local restaurant across the street that tasted so bad we couldn't eat it. It didn't matter, though. Tonight there seemed to be a growing sense of contentment within us.

The night quietly closed in as we went about our evening routine. Cote conversed on Facebook, while I wrote in my journal and mapped out our course for tomorrow's day of driving. We would be passing through Mitchell, South Dakota, the town famous for its great Corn Palace. This was yet another childhood memory of mine tucked away some thirty-odd years ago. I decided to make it the next stop on Cote's rite of passage, and as I refolded our map, I couldn't help but think that it would also be one-stop closer to the lights of home.

Day 12: Motel room in Chamberlain, South Dakota, Midnight

I'll love you forever. I'll like you for always.
As long as I'm living, my baby you'll be.
~Excerpt from *Love You Forever,* by Robert Munsch

An unexpected conversation happened after I closed my journal tonight. It was almost midnight and Cote and I had stayed up much later than usual. With our trip coming to an end, I think subconsciously we were both trying to hang on to what little time we had left. Giving in to sleep would bring morning that much quicker and our rite of passage to an end that much sooner.

Nevertheless, as the midnight hour approached, my resolve to stay awake weakened. I finally set aside my pen and paper and asked Cote if I could switch off the light. To my surprise, her response was to climb out of her own bed and crawl into mine, with actions that mimicked the small, comfort-seeking child she once was years ago. Cote wrapped her arms ferociously around me and buried her head into the crook of my neck. She clung to me as if she were drowning and I was the buoy that would keep her afloat.

"Hey, what's all this?"

"Mom, I wanna tell you something."

"Okay. I'm listening."

Cote then opened a floodgate of emotion that neither of us realized was being held back. She told me how she had just finished exchanging emails with a friend back home, and that they had been talking about relationships, ex-boyfriends in particular. The friend pointed out to Cote that when you're in an unhealthy situation, you risk losing so much other stuff—good stuff—in your life. The friend went on to say, "Unhealthy relationships will consume so much time and energy, that all your healthy ones will get pushed aside, overlooked, neglected."

"When I was dating Brian* this past year and a half, I didn't realize until just now how much it was affecting our relationship. Yours and mine."

"Cote, what are you talking about?"

"Well, I just feel like you and I were fighting more. Maybe not 'fighting' exactly. I don't know. Maybe more just disagreeing. But it was mostly over him."

She went on to tell me that this friend back home reminded Cote just how important family is—much more important than any teenage romance she might ever find herself in. Our family members are the ones in life who truly love us, encourage us, and will always be there for us.

"I see that now," Cote said. "I mean, I always knew it in the back of my mind, you know? But when I was typing my answer back, everything kind of hit me real fast. You've always been there for me, Mom, no matter what. The whole family has been, and I know you guys always will be."

"That's true, Cote. But let me tell you this: you were never going to lose me. Brian or no Brian. I wasn't going anywhere. Yes, we've had our disagreements but your relationship with him was all a part of growing up. I knew that. And when you dealt with what was right and what was wrong in that relationship, you found strength and truth inside yourself. Those are good things, Cote. You learned so much about yourself over the past year and a half. Don't ever forget that."

I held her tight in my arms, and we continued our heart-to-heart. I told her that when the right boy came along, he would not only encourage her relationships with family, he would want to join in them, not pull her away. When that happened—when that certain young man entered her life—her family bonds would then become even stronger.

Cote told me she was excited for a fresh start at Michigan State University, which was only two short weeks away. *How can that be possible?* I told her I was excited for her, too, and that I had a feeling when she stepped onto campus, her life was going to explode with an array of new relationships. "Your life will blossom with friends," I assured her.

We hugged, cried, and talked until after one o'clock in the morning. In a way, I felt Cote finally had the closure she needed regarding her relationship with Brian and what she had left behind. What's more, I knew our relationship as mother and daughter had just been granted an extra protective layering—a kind of security blanket that I could almost physically feel being wrapped around us. We were strong and solid, and ready to cross the threshold of new beginnings. Yet, through all this, we had a firm foundation on which to stand. Cote and I were growing. We were becoming. Together, we were learning to dream bigger and bolder on this rite of passage. Hand in hand, heart-to-heart, I knew we could walk forward into life's unknowns, confident we were up for the challenge. I turned out the light, and offered up a prayer of thankfulness.

NOTE: Name has been changed

Author's Note: In the editing phase of this book, a good friend pointed out to me that the conversation Cote and I had regarding her former boyfriend and her new outlook on relationships, was the direct result of an episode when Cote used technology—the same technology that I had grumbled and griped about earlier in our travels. As I reflected upon this truth, I had to admit my friend was right. Therefore, I would like to recant some of my strong negativity towards Cote's use of electronic devices while on our journey, and admit that I am grateful for the email that sparked our heart-to-heart conversation. To Cote's friend back home, I thank you.

Day 13: Chamberlain, South Dakota to Joliet, Illinois, 746 miles

I soon realized that no journey carries one far unless,
as it extends into the world around us, it goes an equal
distance into the world within.

– Lillian Smith

Cote and I had one of our biggest driving days ever today. We logged well over seven hundred miles, cutting east across the Midwest. We made one quick stop in Mitchell, South Dakota around ten o'clock this morning, to check out the great Corn Palace—a uniquely designed building, which overtime seems to have put this town on the map.

I first came here at the age of twelve, along with my parents and one older brother. All I could remember from that trip was standing in front of the kernel-studded creation and having it be all I could see. Back then the building appeared to sprout out of the ground in the middle of nowhere, huge and monstrous. The word palace seemed fitting, too, as the kernels shimmered in the bright, blazing sunlight. The entire site was wild and exciting for my adolescent brain.

Today, the building was still impressive, but it didn't have quite the same impact on my adult-sized mind. The ambitious undertaking to create such a carousel of corn murals was certainly noteworthy. Looking over the masterpieces, I could appreciate the time and attention it took to construct each and every one.

Every year, the building adopts a new theme, a never-before shucked and shingled showcase of corn-fed art. As Cote and I studied this year's designs, which incorporated thirteen shades of corn and other cropped material, we found it hard to imagine creating such original paintings. What's more, knowing the images would be dismantled and redesigned at the end of every twelve-month cycle, made the project seem a tiny bit crazy to me. Nevertheless, I had to tip my hat to the community's dedication and commitment.

This year, the Corn Palace committee chose a theme tailored-made just for Cote and me—America's Destinations. The scenes were incredibly detailed and to our delight, included both Mount Rushmore and Crazy Horse. We did one walk-through inside the building, bought a few small gifts, and then circled the outer perimeter. We collected a few fallen kernels and small bits of husk caught in the cracks of the sidewalk. These would later be added to our leather-bound journals as keepsakes. Cote and I enjoyed our little side-trek to Mitchell, South Dakota. The town certainly had its very own Field of Dreams—they had built it, and we had come.

The rest of our day was spent driving since our goal was to reach Chicago by nightfall. Every time I reviewed our map, though, the remaining distance indicated we still had a very long way to go.

After we left Mitchell, South Dakota, we jumped back onto I-90 East, the highway that eventually crossed us over the border into Minnesota. Halfway through this Midwest state we turned south on Route 35, with Iowa now our next goal.

At Des Moines, we turned the car eastward onto I-80. For the first time since we'd left home, Cote and I were back on the same stretch of highway that had originally taken us west. As much as we were hoping not to retrace any of our steps during her rite of passage, taking this portion of I-80 made sense. It provided us with the best chance of seeing the Chicago skyline by sundown.

The landscape through these parts was exactly the same as when we had passed through, two weeks earlier. The cornfields were still vast and green. The farmlands were flat and fertile. Cote and I were no longer the same, however. The two of us had grown over the past fourteen days, through our experiences and our discoveries. The trials we had faced made us bolder, less afraid. The triumphs we achieved had given us more confidence and self-assurance.

The atmosphere inside our car had changed over the course of our journey, too. The giddiness we had experienced at our bon voyage had quieted as we sailed smoothly towards our homecoming. Today, Cote and I felt as if we were floating on a calm wave of reflection. Soon our ship would dock on the shores of our Midwestern home, and the two passengers who would disembark would be forever changed by their time away.

As I drove past the quiet, green cornfields, the reality of being inwardly changed sunk deeper and deeper into my psyche. *Can anyone claim to be the exact same person he or she was two weeks ago? Or for that matter, even yesterday?* The roads we choose in life change us. There are times we find ourselves speeding fast down smooth, sleek highways, and other times when dirt roads force us to slow our pace to a mind-crazy crawl. Both routes have their drawbacks—they have pits, potholes, dust, and flying bugs. If we look closely enough, however, we will see they have beauty and blessings as well.

Unexpected rains can wash and renew us. Brilliant rays of sunshine can warm and light the way through the window of our souls. The roads in life may dent and scar us, but they also expand

and define us. There are days we are pushed beyond our limits and times when we're simply stuck along a lonely stretch of back road. Life continues to beckon us forward, however. The path may turn and twist, but when it does, we are often led to new and exciting destinations—places beyond our familiar horizon, to where our hopes and dreams and aspirations lie. The road may not be easy, but it is up to us to mark the miles and make the memories. Then, when the time is right, we can turn and take that one specific route which will lead us home again.

Cote and I could have made it home tonight. By the time we stopped in Juliet, Illinois, we were only four hours from our front doorstep, four hours from the waiting arms of our loved ones. We decided, however, to postpone our homecoming for one more night. Pulling into our driveway at one o'clock in the morning didn't seem fair to our family or right for us. So Cote and I booked one final roadside motel, where we could savor our few remaining hours together.

We couldn't stop the twinge of sadness that settled into our small room, though, as we curled up in front of my laptop to watch a video of our past two weeks together. I had put the clip together using the same songs we had heard and sung along with on our radio ever since we left home—the lyrics having somehow captured the feelings we'd had while on this mother-and-daughter trip of a lifetime.

Cote and I reminisced all our precious moments, laughing, joking and smiling at the memories we made with each passing mile. By midnight, we gave ourselves over to sleep. We sank softly into our beds and into our dreams. It was bittersweet for me to think about Cote's rite of passage coming to an end tomorrow, but I took comfort in knowing there would always be more roads waiting for us up ahead.

Day 14: Joliet, Illinois to Home, 270 miles

Don't cry because it's over. Smile because it happened.
~Dr. Seuss

In all the months leading up to Cote's rite of passage, and even during the past fourteen days, I never gave much thought as to how her trip should or would end. I guess in the back of my mind, I always knew the importance of this mother-daughter journey would be found in the entire two weeks of traveling together; it wasn't about relying on one final hurrah as we crossed the finish line.

When I woke up today, our last morning together, none of this thinking had changed for me. I wasn't hoping for an ultimate gut-wrenching heart-to-heart conversation or one concluding climb to the top of a metaphoric mountain. No grand scenario was rehearsing itself inside my mind, nor did I have any final words of wisdom to impart. Instead, I was ready to simply leave myself open to how this five-thousand-mile mother-daughter journey was supposed to end.

I'm happy to say that what actually—and quite naturally—transpired was the best I could have ever hoped for, far better than anything I could have planned.

During the few remaining hours Cote and I spent together, we rode along in a quiet and knowing consciousness. The miles slipped behind us, slow and easy. We exchanged a few tender smiles, a couple of somber glances, and occasionally we reached across the front seat to squeeze the hand of the other. Every move we made was basic mother-daughter stuff, nothing earth-shattering or time-stopping. The silence we shared cushioned my thoughts, which were focused on our homecoming. *What will it be like when we finally set our bags back down inside the safe and waiting walls of home?* From the look upon my daughter's face, I could tell her thoughts were echoing my own.

Having such a quiet ending to Cote's rite of passage left me a bit stumped about how to write this closing chapter. With no "ah-ha" moment before I turned the car's engine off, how was I to end our story? Could I simply write the truth? That Cote and I pulled into our driveway and stepped into the long awaited, welcoming arms of our family? Would that be enough for you, my reader? Would you accept my words and the story of our journey if I simply wrote, "The End," then set down my pen and walked away?

I finally decided that I could. And that I should. After all, Cote's rite of passage was about the journey we took together, day in and day out. As our time unfolded, we gathered lessons on the art of living. It was just as Cote so eloquently stated back when this idea of a mother-daughter journey first began:

It's not about just showing up and climbing a tree, Mom. It's about seeing everything there is to see along the way. It's about the journey...what it takes to get there. And I want to see it all. I don't want to miss a thing.

Thus, her rite of passage came to be about living, plain and simple. It stood for seeing the beauty in every day given to us, and not being afraid to explore life's possibilities. It was about uncovering a deep well of strength inside and relying on all our senses—sight, smell, sound, and touch—to really experience and appreciate the exquisiteness of our surroundings.

Cote also learned to recognize and listen to the quiet voice inside her, the one that all too often gets drowned out by the repetitive and pounding noises of our world. Her journey became a lesson in what to do and what not to do in life. For example, one should participate, every day, and not just sit on the sidelines warming the bench. Cote also learned there were benefits to be had when saying no—like the times we refused to take the quick and easy routes on our journey, so that we could find the unexpected joys and surprises along the rougher, less direct ones. Cote realized there is a time to play, a time to explore, a time to take risks. And she recognized there are moments to be mindful and walk gently in life; to not push for a faster pace, but instead allow patience and stillness to lead the way.

Cote's rite of passage forced her to acknowledge and accept the truth that fear does exist, but her journey also revealed she possesses a faith that will see her through those dark and scary times. She can confidently step forward into the unknown days ahead with the faith she has in herself, in others, and in a Power greater than any challenge the world may throw at her.

Over these two weeks, Cote tested her instincts and learned that her dreams reside inside the rhythm of her own heart. If she listens carefully enough, she'll be able to follow the path that will take her to them. It won't happen overnight, though. Life isn't played out like a two-hour movie, with one big bang at the end or a major conflict solved before the credits roll.

Life is spent learning how to adjust, reinvent, and even reset your compass when you miss the mark or veer off course. It's about waking up every morning—really waking up—and then noticing the quiet moments that take your breath away. Finally, it's about remembering to always, always, be thankful—even when things don't turn out right. Chances are, if you wait long enough, eventually they will. The outcome may just not be the size or shape you were expecting to find.

In fourteen days, Cote and I traveled far and wide, both inwardly and outwardly. Yet in the end, it was a blessing to come home again. At noon on August 15, 2009, we dropped our duffle bags, and embraced the love and safety waiting for us there. No longer, though, did the word home just mean four walls and a roof. Our time on the road led us to a deeper appreciation, a better understanding. Home is the place where unconditional love resides; the place where the lights are kept well lit, even when you're too far away to see them.

My hope is for Cote to carry this truth with her always. My daughter's next great adventure will be navigated without a close family member by her side. She will leave the security of home alone and set out on a road that will surely be filled with bumps, bad weather, and wrong turns. However, even on her darkest of days, a steady beacon will be shining on the distant horizon, to remind her of the love that is waiting—waiting to embrace and welcome her home.

Epilogue:

The summer of 2011, Cote and I received some very heartbreaking news. Jenny, our tree-climbing companion from California, had returned to the backwoods of Oregon to once again climb the Three Musketeers, the small grove of trees we had ascended together in 2009. To her dismay, Jason told her the three giants were no longer climbable.

The previous winter, a snowstorm had ripped through their area with eighty-five-mile-per-hour winds. The Three Musketeers were hit hard, losing their canopies and their capability of being climbed. Never again would someone sit at the top of these beautiful trees and see the same, incredible views we'd been privy to, and inspired by.

The moment I heard this news, my body went still. I was deeply saddened by the reality of the situation, yet in my state of sorrow, I realized there was one final lesson for me to carry away from Cote's rite of passage:

Time is of the essence. As mothers, we need to take our daughters by the hand and go. Now. Anywhere. Somewhere. We need to take precious time together today, in order to forge the bond of who we are, and who we hope to become. For tomorrow…well, tomorrow may be too late.